Survivors of Eldorado

SURVIVORS OF ELDORADO

FOUR INDIAN CULTURES OF SOUTH AMERICA

Johannes Wilbert

PRAEGER PUBLISHERS
New York · Washington · London

PRAEGER PUBLISHERS
111 Fourth Avenue, New York, N.Y. 10003, U.S.A.
5, Cromwell Place, London SW7 2JL, England

Published in the United States of America in 1972
by Praeger Publishers, Inc.

© 1972 by Praeger Publishers, Inc.

Library of Congress Catalog Card Number: 71-173277

Printed in the United States of America

Contents

Photography and Art Credits

All the line drawings except the one on page 79 are by
Helga Adibi, Saratoga, California. Her work was spon-
sored by the UCLA-CLAVE Venezuelan Indian Project.
The drawing on page 79 is by José Luis Ulibarrena, Sociedad de Ciencias Naturales La Salle, Caracas.

Sources of photographs are as follows:

YANOAMA
   Nos. 1, 4, 6, 8 Barbara Brändli, Venezuela. UCLA-
   CLAVE Venezuelan Indian Project
   Nos. 2, 3, 5, 7 Karl Weidmann, Venezuela

WARAO

Nos. 1, 2, 8 Johannes Wilbert, University of California. UCLA-CLAVE Venezuelan Indian Project

Nos. 3, 4, 5, 6, 7 Peter T. Furst, State University of New York, Albany. UCLA-CLAVE Venezuelan Indian Project

MAKIRITARE

No. 1 Fundación La Salle de Ciencias Naturales, Venezuela

Nos. 2, 3, 4, 5, 6, 7, 8 Barbara Brändli, Venezuela. UCLA-CLAVE Venezuelan Indian Project

GOAJIRO

Nos. 1, 4, 5, 6, 7, 8 Walter Wachter, Lichtenstein

Nos. 2, 3 H. Homer Aschmann, University of California

Preface

The four Indian societies discussed in this book were chosen because they represent four types of adaptation (hunting, fishing, horticulture, and cattle herding) and because they are relatively well documented. They are also among the few surviving aboriginal cultures in northern South America whose traditional systems, although under increasing pressure from the dominant Creole culture, either are still relatively intact (Yanoama, Warao, Makiritare) or have undergone peaceful change in response to new traits and conditions introduced after the Conquest (Goajiro). In marked contrast, many hundreds of other indigenous groups were unable to withstand or adapt to the radical transformation of the South American continent after 1492 and became culturally and physically extinct.

For centuries the great Spanish friar Bartolomé de Las Casas was derided as a liar for charging 20 million Indian lives to the Spanish Conquest; today we know that his statistics may not have been so far off the mark after all. The best estimates now place the aboriginal population of the Americas as a whole at no less than 100 million in 1492. South of Panama alone, the fifteenth-century aboriginal population is estimated at 49 million. But, within a few decades after Columbus' first voyage, only an estimated

2 million Indians were left alive in South America—a loss of 96 per cent of the original total! We know from Spanish colonial sources that, in the first few decades of the Conquest and colonization, nineteen out of every twenty Indians in Mexico fell victim to disease, slavery, forced labor, or murder, as well as loss of the will to live under the spiritual and physical conditions imposed by the Europeans. In all, an estimated 90 million to 95 million of the original 100 million who made their lives as hunters, fishermen, or cultivators between the Arctic and the Tierra del Fuego have become extinct in the past four hundred years.

As Las Casas charged and as has since been confirmed by distinguished historians, the most precipitous decline occurred in the Caribbean and along the tropical coasts of South America. Along the northern littoral the "undeclared war" against the Indians began with the first *entradas* up the Orinoco and out of Coro, whose chief objective was discovery of the fabled Eldorado somewhere in the Meta region, in the mountainous hinterlands of Coro, or in the Cordilleras east and west of Lake Maracaibo. In many areas of the Venezuelan "slave coast" the entire native population was wiped out within a short time after initial European contact. Today hardly a trace of Indian life remains from Cumaná in the east to Maracaibo in the west, a region that was heavily settled in aboriginal times.

The Indians possessed no effective means of defense against the powerful and ruthless European invaders, no means even of escape, except where nature provided sanctuary. In the more rugged areas, some Indians managed to flee into the most inaccessible reaches of the Cordilleras, where, as the German conquistador Federmann himself was forced to admit, "one could not follow them on cats, let alone horses," into the waterless deserts, the swamps, and the deepest jungle. Of those tribes that could find no route of escape and no refuge, most perished altogether in the course of the initial Conquest.

The ancestors of our four sample societies were among the fortunate tribes who found refuge in the inaccessible desert (Goajiro), the jungle (Yanoama, Makiritare), or the swamps (Warao) and thus became survivors of the Eldorado obsession of the Conquistadors. The cultures of these Indians represent rather characteristic examples of the cultural levels achieved by the aborigines of lowland South America: the Paleo-Indian hunters and gatherers, the Meso-Indian fishermen, and the Neo-Indian horticulturalists. The development of cattle herding among the Goajiro is, of course, an adaptation unique among American Indians.

The selected tribes and their cultures should by no means be taken as "stages" of cultural achievement in a unilinear evolutionist scheme; it is true that, nevertheless, there is a kind of continuum from the Yanoama, who, as hunters and collectors of wild food, appear to be one of the last examples of the way of life that was general throughout the Americas before the advent of food cultivation, to the Goajiro, who provide an interesting example of cultural malleability and peaceful adaptation to new conditions. The Warao, a traditional swamp and riverine fishing society, and the Makiritare, with their age-old system of slash-and-burn yuca cultivation, fall somewhere between these two extremes.

The descriptions of these four societies were written more or less in the "ethnographic present"—that is, as they were observed by ethnographers in the past several decades. However, even among these remote societies, many new traits have been replacing traditional ones, and not just in the material sphere. Settlement patterns, material culture, the food quest, even ideology are undergoing heavy and accelerating pressure for change. Thus, while these four "type"-societies are exceptional in that they

have retained much of their aboriginal culture, they do so
under continuous adaptation.

The cultural summaries in this book are based on my
own field experience but also, to a much larger extent, on
the work of many other ethnographers. I had at my disposal an extensive file on Venezuelan Indians, which includes the writings of hundreds of authors. Although I
cannot list them individually here, I feel greatly indebted
to their work and herewith acknowledge their contribution, which looms so large in this book.* At the end of
each chapter I have listed only those books and articles
that I had to lean on most heavily as indispensable sources of
unique information, especially in the case of Barandiarán's
Yanoama and Makiritare papers. All these documents
should be consulted by anyone interested in going beyond
the introductory level of this book. Also included are lists
of several immensely valuable ethnographic films on the
tribes discussed.

The present book has been prepared as a contribution to
"La Condición Humana en America Latina," a project
designed to examine the conditions of human life in Latin
America and to appraise the prospects of its further development. Sponsors of the project are the Centro de Estudios
del Futuro de Venezuela, Universidad Católica Andres
Bello (Caracas); the Centre International pour le Dévelop-
pement (Paris); and the Latin American Center at UCLA
(University of California, Los Angeles). Through the Centro Latino-americano de Venezuela, the Creole Foundation

* A comprehensive bibliography of Venezuelan Indians was published
by Helmuth Fuchs, *Bibliografía Básica de Etnología de Venezuela,* Universidad de Sevilla, Publicaciones del Seminario de Antropología Americana,
V, Seville, 1964. See also Timothy J. O'Leary, *Ethnographic Bibliography
of South America,* Human Relations Area Files, Behavior Science Bib-
liographies, New Haven, 1953; Gerardo Reichel-Dolmatoff, "Bibliografía
de La Guajira," *Revista de la Academia de Ciencias Exactas, Físicas y
Naturales,* VII, No. 45 (1963), 41–56.

has made available a grant in support of research assistance. Charlotte Treuenfels was kind enough to edit the first drafts of the book. Professor Peter T. Furst, my friend and former colleague at the UCLA Latin American Center, edited the final version. His erudition and unfailing encouragement have greatly enhanced the study and speeded its completion.

Los Angeles, California
October, 1971

Survivors of Eldorado

1 The Indians of Venezuela

Man did not originate in America. Some 20,000 years ago there were probably no human beings in that part of South America now politically defined as Venezuela. The first inhabitants of Venezuela were descendants of Asiatic peoples, immigrants into North America via the Siberia–Chukchi land bridge, between 50,000 and 35,000 years ago, before the Bering Sea passage was temporarily blocked. The remote ancestors of our Indians moved slowly through what are now Alaska, Canada, the United States, Mexico, and Central America, eventually reaching northern South America.

We call these first immigrants Paleo-Americans, to distinguish them from Neo-Americans, the descendants of a second major wave of immigrants who crossed into the New World when the Bering Strait again became passable, beginning perhaps 25,000 years ago, toward the end of and following the last ice age. It is possible that the Paleo-Americans were of a generalized Caucasoid origin, a type still represented in Asia by such remnant populations as the Ainu of northern Japan, whereas the Neo-Americans might have been predominantly of a generalized Mongoloid racial type. This, however, remains hypothetical. In any event, the descendants of the Neo-American immi-

3

CULTURAL DEVELOPMENT IN VENEZUELA

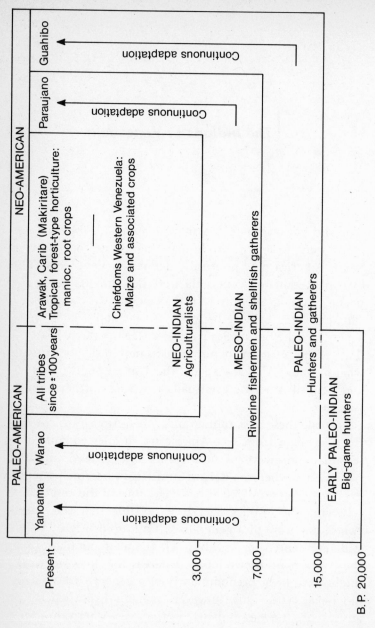

Figure 1

grants reached Venezuela possibly 20,000 years ago (Figure 1).

Both the Paleo-Americans and the Neo-Americans developed Paleo-Indian hunting and Meso-Indian fishing cultures. To us these may look very much alike, but they have their roots in quite different depths of human development. Specialized Meso-Indian fishing cultures developed only about 7,000 years ago. So far as we can see, only Neo-Americans developed a Neo-Indian type of food-growing economy. However, most surviving Paleo-Americans adopted horticulture sometime during the last century.

At the time of the Conquest, some 500 years ago, there was great linguistic diversity among Venezuelan aborigines. There is evidence of more than 110 Venezuelan Indian languages and dialects, belonging to ten different stocks. Granted that a large percentage of these are dialects rather than mutually unintelligible languages, the number of idioms nevertheless remains impressive. Of the ten stocks extant in post-Conquest Venezuela (Arawakan, Cariban, Chibchan, Guamoan, Jirajaran, Otomacan, Piaroan, Timotean, Waraoan, and Yanoaman), four (Guamoan, Jirajaran, Otomacan, Timotean) are extinct or virtually extinct. However, at least 20 representative languages of the remaining six stocks persist (Figure 2).

1. The *Arawakan* languages include Goajiro, Paraujano, Piapoco, Curipaco, Guahibo (with Cuiva), and Bare-Baniva.
2. The *Cariban* languages include Yupa (with markedly differing dialects, viz.: Irapa, Shaparu, Pariri, Ovabre, Macoita, Japreria, *et al.*), Yabarana (with Orechicano and Guaiquiare), Panare, Yecuana, Pemon (with Taurepan, Arecuna, and Camaracoto), and Cariña.
3. The *Chibchan* languages include Barí and Yaruro (and possibly also Warao and Yanoama).

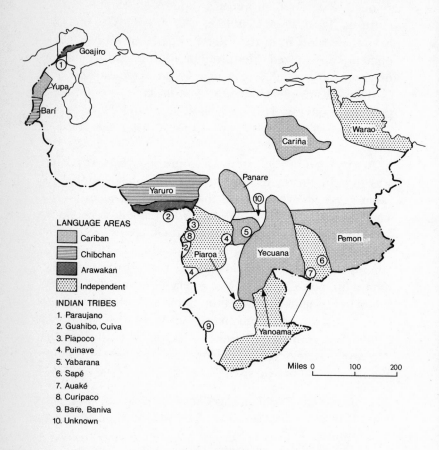

LINGUISTIC AFFILIATION OF VENEZUELAN INDIANS
APPROXIMATE EXTENSION OF LANGUAGE AREAS

Goajiro

Yupa

Barí

Warao

Cariña

Yaruro

Panare

Pemon

Piaroa

Yecuana

Yanoama

LANGUAGE AREAS

Cariban
Chibchan
Arawakan
Independent

INDIAN TRIBES
1. Paraujano
2. Guahibo, Cuiva
3. Piapoco
4. Puinave
5. Yabarana
6. Sapé
7. Auaké
8. Curipaco
9. Bare, Baniva
10. Unknown

Miles 0   100   200

Figure 2

4. *Piaroan* includes the dialects of Macó and Sáliva.
5. *Waraoan* has several slightly differing dialects such as Mariusa, Winikina, and Guayo (possibly of Chibchan stock).
6. *Yanoaman* includes various different dialects and languages: Sanemá, Waika, Samatari, and others (possibly of Chibchan stock).

Sapé (Kaliana) and Auaké are little-known isolated languages that are practically extinct. Other languages spoken in an as yet unexplored region of Territorio Amazonas remain completely unknown. The small enclave of Puinave speakers are of Macúan affiliation.

Today these languages are spoken by less than a score of Venezuelan Indian tribes who continue to function according to autochthonous patterns. A study of such type-cultures as the Yanoama (hunters), the Warao (fishermen), the Makiritare (horticulturists), and the Goajiro (cattle herders) will give us as accurate a picture as is currently possible of aboriginal life in Venezuela. The culture levels of the tribes in our sample and those of some other Indian groups can be roughly categorized according to the scheme of Table 1.

Cultural schematization of this kind is always unsatisfactory, inasmuch as horticulturists also hunt or fish, hunters also fish, and fishermen also hunt. Nevertheless, the scheme does register the predominant food-quest activities of each tribe and the concomitant overall cultural levels. Cultures like those of the Otomac and Timote were even more advanced than those of the Neo-Indian horticulturists listed. Unfortunately, during the five hundred years of the Indo-Hispanic period, these formative cultures succumbed to the impact of European settlers and have since disappeared. Their cultural heritage is lost forever, and any survivors have been absorbed into a Neo-Venezuelan Cre-

Table 1

CONTEMPORANEOUS VENEZUELAN INDIANS AND THEIR
CULTURAL TYPES*

Paleo-Indian Hunters	Meso-Indian Fishermen	Neo-Indian Horticulturists	Neo-Indian Cattle Herders
Guahibo (Cuiva)	Paraujano	Yupa	Goajiro
Yanoama	Yaruro	Barí	
	Warao	Piaroa	
		Panare	
		Yabarana	
		Makiritare (Yecuana)	
		Bare-Baniva	
		Sapé, Auaké	
		Pemon	
		Cariña	

* Several splinter groups of predominantly Colombian tribes are excluded.

ole culture. Those tribes that remain, their geographical distribution, and approximate total population figures are shown in Figure 3 and Table 2.

DISTRIBUTION OF VENEZUELAN INDIAN TRIBES
APPROXIMATE TOTAL POPULATION

1 . Goajiro
2 . Paraujano
3 . Yupa
4 . Barí
5 . Guahibo, Cuiva
6 . Yaruro
7 . Piaroa (Macó)
8 . Panare
9 . Yabarana
10 . Yecuana
11 . Piapoco
12 . Curipaco
13 . Puinave
14 . Bare, Baniva
15 . Yanoama
16 . Sapé, Auaké
17 . Pemon
18 . Warao
19 . Cariña

Figure 3

Table 2

ADJUSTED DEMOGRAPHIC FIGURES ON THE INDIAN POPULATION OF VENEZUELA

Tribe	No.	Habitat	Source of Information
1. Goajiro a	8,429	Peninsula La Guajira	National Census, 1960
2. Paraujano	1,348	Sinamaica Lagoon	National Malaria Service, 1958
3. Yupa b	2,176	Northern Sierra de Perijá	Ruddle, 1971 (personal communication)
4. Barí c	1,000	Southern Sierra de Perijá	Lizarralde, 1964 (personal communication)
5. Yaruro	1,427	Between the Arauca and Meta rivers	National Census, 1960
6. Guahibo (Cuiva)	5,397	Meta River, Middle Orinoco River	National Census, 1960
7. Piaroa (Macó)	1,886	Arch of the Orinoco River	National Census, 1960
8. Panare	412	Llanos of Caicara, Cuchivero River	Wilbert, 1963
9. Yabarana	64	Manapiare River	National Census, 1960
10. Makiritare (Yecuana)	1,200	Caura, Ventuari, Cunucunuma rivers	Mission Petits Frères, 1965 (personal communication)
11. Piapoco	99	Middle Orinoco River	National Census, 1960
12. Curipaco	212	Middle Orinoco, Ventuari rivers	National Census, 1960
13. Puinave	240	Atabapo, Orinoco rivers	National Census, 1960
14. Bare-Baniva	645	Southern Territorio Amazonas	National Census, 1960

	Tribe	No.	Habitat	Source of Information
15.	Yanoama	10,000	Territorio Amazonas (i.e., excluding Yanoama of Brazil	Rough estimate, Chagnon, 1968
16.	Sapé, Auaké	100	Antabari, Pao, Paragua rivers	Rough estimate
17.	Pemon *d*	2,700	Gran Sabana	National Census, 1960
18.	Warao *e*	12,000	Orinoco Delta	Capuchin Mission, 1968
19.	Cariña	3,728	Anzoátegui State	Schwerin, 1966
20.	Unknown *f*	1,000	Sierra Guamapi	Rough estimate
	Total	54,063	(Less than 1% of the total population of Venezuela)	

a According to the National Census of Colombia, there were 44,748 Goajiro Indians in 1951. Of these, only 8,429 seemed to live in Venezuelan territory.

b This figure includes an estimated 692 Yupa (Yuco) on the Colombian side of the Sierra de Perijá. (Ruddle, personal communication, 1971.)

c This estimated figure includes the Colombian Barí. Pinton (1965, p. 254) considers her figure of 7,600 for the same year as possibly exaggerated.

d Including the Taurepan, Arecuna, and Camaracoto.

e This figure may have to be increased by 2,000 or even 3,000 as of 1970.

f This includes an unknown tribe in the Sierra as well as the so-called Monteros, who are kin of the Yabarana.

BIBLIOGRAPHY

Chagnon, Napoleon A., *Yanomamö: The Fierce People: Case Studies in Cultural Anthropology*. New York: Holt, Rinehart & Winston, 1968.

Cruxent, J. M., and I. Rouse, *An Archeological Chronology of Venezuela*. Social Science Monograph, VI. Washington, D.C.: Pan American Union, 1958.

Dobyns, Henry F., "Estimating Aboriginal American Populations," *Current Anthropology*, VII, 4 (Oct., 1966), 395-416.

Loukotka, Cestmír, *Classification of South American Indian Languages*. Reference Series, VII. Los Angeles: Latin American Center, University of California, Los Angeles, 1968.

Pinton, Solange, "Les Bari," *Journal de la Société des Américanistes*, LIV, 2 (1967), 247-333. Paris.

Reichel-Dolmatoff, Gerardo, "Contribución al Conocimiento de las Tribus de la Región de Perijá," *Revista Colombiana de Antropología*, IX (1960), 159-98. Bogotá.

Sanoja, Mario, "Cultural Development in Venezuela," in *Aboriginal Cultural Development in Latin America: An Interpretative Review*. Smithsonian Miscellaneous Collections, CXLVI, 1 (1963), 67-76. Washington, D.C.

Schwerin, Karl H., *Oil and Steel*. Latin American Studies, IV. Los Angeles: University of California, Los Angeles, 1966.

Wilbert, Johannes, "Cultural Variability in Venezuelan Indian Tribes," in Francisco M. Salzano, ed., *The Ongoing Evolution of Latin American Populations*. Springfield, Ill.: Charles C. Thomas, 1971, pp. 127-59.

———, *Indios de la Región Orinoco-Ventuari*. Caracas: Fundación La Salle de Ciencias Naturales, Monografías, No. 8, 1963.

2 The Hunters: The Yanoama of Territorio Amazonas

The early Venezuelans were Paleo-Indian hunters who invaded the country in pursuit of Pleistocene game.* They pushed all the way across the land to the mouth of the Orinoco and northward to the Caribbean. The temperature was then lower than it is today, and Trinidad was still connected to the mainland. In addition to obtaining meat from such Pleistocene big game as the mammoth, glyptodon, giant sloth, camel, and horse, they probably also collected wild vegetable foods, especially palm fruits, in the dense forests that covered much of the now denuded area of the country. Seafood seems to have offered less attraction to the Paleo-Indians, and riverine fishing, if practiced at all, was probably of little moment. The tool kit of these hunters included quartzite choppers and scrapers, bifacially worked blades—which might have been used as spear points, axes, or knives—and lanceolate projectile points that were probably used as heads for spears that may have been hurled by a mechanical spear thrower rather than by the unassisted hand. No doubt, variants of the general culture type developed in response to new habitats, but the

* The archaeological data in this book were largely taken from I. Rouse and J. M. Cruxent, *Venezuelan Archaeology*, Caribbean Studies, VI, Yale University Press, New Haven, Conn.: 1963.

focus remained on hunting land animals and on improving the technology and organization of local groups to ensure their survival.

The Paleo-Indian epoch of Venezuela lasted for possibly 13,000 years, from 20,000 to 7,000 B.P. (before present). Following the first wave of immigrants, new peoples arrived in Venezuela during this time. These later Paleo-Indian arrivals probably included descendants of the second major wave of Asiatic immigrants to the New World, those who crossed the Siberia–Chukchi land bridge during the late Wisconsin glacial advances, between 25,000 and 12,000 years ago.

Among the contemporary Indian tribes of Venezuela, we can identify the Yanoama of the Territorio Amazonas as having continued the pre-agricultural Paleo-Indian hunting tradition. Only very recently have they adopted horticulture. They are expert hunters but also rely heavily on palm fruits to supplement their diet. Fishing, where practiced at all, plays a secondary role. The men carry detachable arrowheads of bamboo in their quivers and make lanceolate points, such as those found in several Meso-Indian sites in Venezuela. The Guahibo (Cuiva) may also be surviving Paleo-Indian cultures, although physically they seem to indicate a different origin.*

It is an astonishing fact that the one Indian group whose way of life today is most like that of all Indians in the tropics before the introduction of agriculture also survives as one of the largest and most successful autochthonous

---

* By calling these tribes survivors of the old-time hunters in Venezuela, we do not mean to imply that they are physically and culturally identical to the hunters of 20,000 years ago. The body type and culture of a people undergo constant changes, for neither time nor human development stands still. By "Paleo-Indian survivors" we mean, rather, a surviving *type* hunting culture, which, in spite of continuous adaptation, exhibits a set of distinctive socio-economic, technical, and ideological characteristics. The same is also true of Meso- and Neo-Indian survivors.

populations in lowland South America. Population estimates for the Yanoama vary from 25,000 to 40,000; the
lower figure is probably more nearly correct, but it is still
very impressive. The survival of Yanoama in such substantial numbers contrasts sharply with the near obliteration
of other Neo-Indian lowland agriculturalists; it is interesting also in view of the seemingly endemic intergroup warfare and occasional violent individual behavior among the
Yanoama, which have been the focus of much recent
anthropological interest.* When we consider the large
number of Yanoama and remember that much of the Upper Orinoco is now virtually devoid of animal life, we
cannot help but wonder whether the characteristic type of
Yanoama warfare (which usually results in few fatalities),
combined with female infanticide, constitutes a historical-
evolutionary mechanism to keep the population in balance
with available resources. In any event, as we shall see, preoccupation with male bravery in combat and its symbols
runs through much of Yanoama cultural behavior.

THE HABITAT

The Yanoama inhabit an extensive area—some 15,000
square kilometers—between 0° 30′ and 5° North latitude
and 62°-65° West longitude. Straddling the frontier between Venezuela and Brazil, this region encompasses
the headwaters of several important rivers—the Paragua,
Ventuari, Padamo, Ocamo, Mavaca, and Orinoco in Venezuela, and the Uraricuera, Catrimani, Dimini, and Aracá
in Brazil. The Sierra Parima crosses this heavily forested,
humid, and hot country like a kind of vertebral column,
at the same time marking the frontier between the Venezuelan and the Brazilian parts of Yanoama-land. Of the

* See especially Napoleon A. Chagnon, "Yanomamö Social Organization
and Warfare," in "War: The Anthropology of Armed Conflict and Aggression," *Natural History*, LXXVI, pp. 40-70. December 1, 1967.

total Yanoama population, perhaps 10,000 live in Venezuela and another 15,000-20,000 in Brazil. With Cariban
tribes enclosing them in a semicircle to the northeast and
Arawakans in a semicircle to the southwest, the Yanoama
seem to have functioned as a buffer between these two
groups, at the same time successfully resisting intrusion
into their territory by either tribe. The Yanoama as a
whole consist of a number of distinguishable subtribes,
including the Sanemá, the Waika, and the Samatari. White
contact occurred only recently; most of our knowledge of
Yanoama culture was accumulated by missionaries, ethnol-
ogists, and travelers during the last forty years.

LANGUAGE

Very early in the course of these surveys and investiga-
tions, it became apparent that the language of the Yanoama
was not related to any of the major tropical-forest language
families—Arawakan, Cariban, or Tupian. Most ethnol-
ogists continue to consider Yanoaman an independent
tongue, possibly related to earlier South American languages that have become extinct. In recent years, however,
the whole problem of Yanoaman taxonomy has had to be
reopened as a result of new classificatory efforts by compe-
tent linguists who contend that in fact Yanoaman is related
to Chibchan. This came as a distinct surprise, because
Chibchan languages are distributed mainly through the
highlands of northwestern South America, rather than the
lowlands. Recent comparative linguistic work on Waraoan
in the Orinoco Delta turned up the same Chibchan affiliation, a point to which we will return in the next chapter.
In any event, Yanoaman and Waraoan, once held to represent independent stocks, are now considered by some linguists to be related to highland Chibchan, and consequently
also to each other. However, any current linguistic relationship between these two lowland Chibchan languages, on

the one hand, and highland Chibchan, on the other, appears to be quite remote. It is possible that such cognate relations as are still perceivable are based on a formerly shared language, which, in the case of highland Chibchan, was largely blanketed by the language of more recent intruders into the highlands.

Internal linguistic variation is quite pronounced among speakers of Yanoaman, ranging from simple dialectic variations to more profound differences, and possibly different languages. For example, the Sanemá seem to have considerable difficulty in conversing with the Waika. Nevertheless, communication is possible even among geographically extremely separated groups, and if different tongues have developed within the Yanoaman stock, they must be of fairly recent origin.

MATERIAL CULTURE AND TECHNOLOGY

Yanoama technology is little developed and lacks most of the landmarks of more advanced Neo-Indian food-growing cultures of the tropical forest. As a result, the material culture inventory of these Indians is so meager that it is hard to imagine how any society could have endured in such poverty. But endure they did, and they continue to do so most effectively. Indeed, they clearly demonstrate the fallacy of defining "underdevelopment" in terms of a single cultural aspect, for to do so in this case would mean to ignore their richly developed system of values and beliefs and their remarkably successful adaptation to their forest environment, which have enabled them to survive as a cohesive culture over untold millenniá to the present day.

Clothing is virtually absent. Like many other peoples of South America, the Yanoama adorn the body more than they clothe it; aesthetic and magico-religious values outweigh practical considerations. During the first few years of childhood, Yanoama boys and girls go naked. Thereafter both sexes wear various kinds of body ornaments and paints. Indispensable, however, is a waist string of either vegetable fiber or homespun cotton. Men fasten the prepuce of the penis to their string, and both sexes consider it quite embarrassing to be seen without a waist string. On festive

Belts of cotton thread, worn by Yanoama men (*left*) and women (*right*). (*After Becher*)

occasions, men, women, and children wear a belt of cotton yarn over the string. Belts for men and boys are thin and round, those for females flat and wide. The ends of the belt do not quite join in front but leave a free space and are held together with a string. The belts are dyed red with onoto (a red vegetable dye), and often they are also painted with meanders, circles, and dots. Some women tie the ends of their loosely wound cotton belt in front with a short, fringed string. This apron-like part of the belt may be deco- rated with bird feathers and shells. Some adults, and many

children, wear strips of jaguar hide around their waist as
protection from sickness and danger. Yanoama women also
wear a long, continuous string or roll of strings crosswise
around the torso. Like the waist string and belt, these are
made of vegetable fiber or cotton yarn and are either uni-
formly dyed red or decorated with rings of onoto paint.
In addition, women wear cotton string around their upper
arms and wrists as well as around their legs, below the
knees and at the ankles. Men usually wear bands of cotton
string only around their upper arms; on festive occasions,
these are replaced by ribbons of animal skin and bird
feathers. Long ornaments of macaw, turkey, heron, and
hawk feathers are sometimes fastened to the armbands of
the men by cotton string.

Colorful feathers of every kind of bird figure prom-
inently as ornaments for the men. The women keep their
husbands' plumed ornaments in special boxes made of
bark. On festive occasions, when there is dancing, the men
may glue the white down feathers of the harpy eagle or
king vulture all over their heads, somewhat resembling a
feather cap or, especially when a monkey tail is wound
around the forehead, a crown. The fine monkey tails are
dried and tied with a string at the base and the tip. Fastened to the tail are pieces of cotton, from the lower ends
of which dangle colorful bunches of feathers. Another
specifically male decoration is a bracelet hung all over with
little sticks. Besides other distinguishing ornaments, such
bracelets, together with small sticks in the earlobes, mark
the warrior who has killed an enemy. In a number of subtribes, bird feathers are also worn by women, who insert
them into holes below the lower lip and at the corners of
the mouth. More commonly, however, women use slender
rods for this purpose. Flowers are worn in perforations in
the earlobe. Men also decorate their pierced earlobes with
feathers. The women of several Yanoama subtribes char-

acteristically wear long, slender, white shafts through the septum of the nose. During or at some time prior to puberty, women perforate the corners of their lips, the middle of the lower lip, the septum, and the earlobes. A pijiguao (peach-palm) thorn is used to puncture the corners of the mouth; the lips, nose, and ears are pierced with an awl of bacaba wood. Some woods are known to the Yanoama to cause inflammation when used for this purpose, and the points of bacaba awls are scorched prophylactically to avoid such complications.

The adults as well as the children of most Yanoama sub-tribes cut their hair short around the head with a wide tonsure on the crown. The size of the tonsure varies from group to group, but the Sanemá, a northern subtribe, deviate from this hair style altogether. Instead, they keep a full head of hair trimmed short at equal length all around, but without a tonsure. Shaving the tonsure and cutting the hair are accomplished by means of a grass blade or a split and sharpened piece of reed. The clean-shaven tonsure is frequently painted red with onoto. Warriors who have killed an enemy refrain for some time from cutting their hair and painting their tonsure. The skin of the tonsure of the men is usually deeply scarred as a result of club blows in duels, in which the skull cap of the opponent is the main target.

Body painting is of great importance to the adult Yano-ama, serving either for decoration, for reasons of etiquette, or for more transcendent purposes of a magico-religious nature. Some forty different patterns of body painting have been recorded, mostly symbolic representations of the fauna and flora of Yanoama-land. Onoto is the principal dye used, but a black paint is also produced by mixing saliva, tears, or water with charcoal, the ashes of certain resins, and the ashes of the dead.

Red is the color of life and happiness. Both sexes paint

their entire body red with onoto. Visitors paint themselves
with this color before entering the village of their hosts.
Guests who come painted red, or with fine red and black
lines, come as friends and thus announce their peaceable
intentions. Only people visiting members of their own
subtribe consider it superfluous to apply body paint before
entering another's village. A young woman leaving the
seclusion of her first menstruation re-enters the village
with her body painted red or pink.

Black is the color of death, warfare, and mourning. Warriors paint their entire bodies black before engaging the
enemy. A man painted black inspires awe and portrays the
Yanoama ideal of fearless bravery. Parents even paint their
small sons black to ensure their future valor. Men and
women paint themselves black before conducting funeral
rituals, such as preparing the corpse for cremation or consuming the ashes of the bones of their dead. The women
prepare a black paint of tears and charcoal which they apply to their cheeks and which remains there for months as
a sign of mourning. Especially durable is the black paint
made for the same purpose of a mixture of resin, ashes of
the bones of the defunct, and onoto. Only after the ashes
of the dead have been consumed, during the annual death
ceremony, do the women remove the black facial paint of
mourning.

Red, dark blue, and black dyes are also used to paint
fairly common designs of straight lines, wavy lines, and geo-
metric patterns over the entire body. Several Yanoama
subtribes use genipapo, another vegetable dye, to tattoo
small dots in the form of a declining semicircle across the
upper lips of girls undergoing their first menstruation. The
body of such a girl is painted pink with a light cover of
onoto over which black wavy lines are drawn. Some of the
Yanoama designs of body painting are recognized as sug-
gestive of the skin and fur ornamentations of animals

hunted or feared by them. Animal designs and symbols of bush spirits are also prescribed by the shamans on ceremonial occasions and a relationship exists between designs of body painting and the shaman's tutelary spirits, which are commonly conceived of as animal. The Yanoama hunter seeks to establish a propitious relationship with the supernatural guardians of animal species by painting his body with an appropriate species symbol.

Roaming swiftly through his extensive hunting territory, a Yanoama travels light, with a minimum of utensils and tools. Basketry is quite poorly developed, even though carrying and storage baskets are of immense importance to these seminomadic forest people. A large U-shaped carrying basket is used by the women with a tumpline of bast to transport heavy loads of firewood, garden products, utensils, and even babies. Dish-like baskets are used to store cotton and fruits and as sieves for straining the ashes of the bones of the dead. Several other basketry types found sporadically throughout the Yanoama territory are of foreign origin. A large circular tray, for instance, used by the women for fishing in shallow streams, is a poor imitation of a piece of basketry rather typical of their Neo-Indian neighbors. Basketry is clearly identified with the domain of the Yanoama woman. She collects the fine liana that serves as raw material, splits the strands, and produces both the carrying basket and the dish-like storage basket in the twining technique, a mode characteristically archaic among South American Indians. After the basket is completed, the weaver paints it with onoto and decorates it with wavy lines and dots in each of the curves. She may ask her husband to apply the decoration. Otherwise, a man does not want to be associated with such "woman's work," and considers it a grave insult should someone suggest that he is more fit to carry a basket than a bow.

Split liana strands, roughly 2 meters in length, are used

to make a primitive hammock of a kind that is uniquely Yanoaman. To produce it, a man or woman will simply gather a handful of liana strands by splitting a vine and cutting the strands with the teeth to body length. The ends are firmly tied together with the same material and reinforced by intertwining a bast rope below the binding on each end. Occasionally, the liana strands of this hammock are loosely joined by traverse lianas or cotton threads. The finished product is often painted with onoto. Liana hammocks of this kind, including suspension ropes of the same material, can be produced in a very short time, so that the women do not always bother to carry them along in their baskets when the family moves over great distances.

The decision whether to take or leave the hammock behind is even simpler in the case of the hammock of bast. A more primitive form of hammock than this cannot be imagined. Men make them, after pitching camp, by simply walking up to an emvira tree and tearing off a sizable piece of bark. If the tree is large it will supply enough bark to make hammocks for the whole family. A bast hammock may be made of a single strip of bark or of multiple strips, knotted to a suspension rope of the same material on either end. Baby slings are made of a band of the same bast 5 to 10 centimeters wide.

Hammocks made of cotton thread have recently become more common among several Yanoama subtribes, whose women learned to make them from their Neo-Indian neighbors, especially the Makiritare, or else obtained them by barter. This type of cotton hammock is made by winding cotton strings around two sturdy upright poles, spaced according to the length desired. The strings are joined at wide intervals by traverse braided threads. The suspension ropes are also made of cotton strings. According to the Yanoama, the hummingbirds were the first to have cotton hammocks. Before they changed from humans into birds they taught the Yanoama how to plant cotton, spin, and make cotton-thread hammocks. But even today there are a few Yanoama groups that neither plant cotton nor spin cotton string. Spinning is woman's work. They spin thread with a spindle made of a 40-centimeter-long rodlet or a leaf stem with a disk-like whorl of wood or bone. The product is used for the manufacture of belts and other body ornaments. Balls of cotton thread are also an important item of trade. But weaving remains an unknown art among the Yanoama, and looms of any sort are completely absent.

Pottery is practiced by only a few communities of several subtribes, such at the Waika, Samatari, and Karimé. These groups produce a crude, conical cooking pot with a 2-centimeter-thick round bottom and tapering walls.

Yanoama clay pots.

The rim is very thin, and the entire vessel, badly fired as it is, breaks easily. Women make these vessels by the coil technique, building the pot slowly by superimposing slender rolls of clay, flattened inside and outside the pot. After allowing the soft clay vessel to dry slowly in the shade, the women fire it under a pile of brush and wood. These heavy and brittle cooking pots are actually quite impractical for a highly mobile life. It is usually the old men who carry them on the march, strapped to their backs, possibly together with the liana hammocks of the family.

In the absence of earthenware pots, the men make a cooking vessel of bark tied together with lianas. The same bark is also used to produce large troughs for the plantain soup consumed on festive occasions. Bark cooking pots are apparently made only by men, who must avoid looking at a pregnant woman at the time of manufacture, since this causes the bark to break. Men are also the only ones to use these bark containers for cooking fruits. Women get distracted too easily, they maintain, and let the fire burn through the bark. Widows who lack an earthenware cooking pot sometimes resort to cooking foods on small pieces of bark, which they send the children to fetch for them.

As one would suspect, metal pots and metal goods in general are absent from indigenous Yanoama material culture. Instead there is eager trading for metal cooking pots, containers, axes, cutlass-like machetes, knives, and scissors with the Creoles or with Yanoama groups that have established contact with civilization. Traditional cutting tools are slivers of grass, pieces of split bamboo or reed, the lower part of a tortoise shell, the canine teeth of wild boars, or knives made from the lower incisor of the agouti, a rabbit-sized rodent also known as acure. The long, slender, and slightly curved agouti tooth has a sharp edge and is fastened at its base to a short piece of wood by means of resin adhesive and string. The tool is used as a chisel, mainly for whittling the lanceolate arrowheads from bamboo. The men carry one or two of these agouti-tooth knives attached to their arrowhead quivers.

Attached to the same quiver is the fire-drill, which consists of two pieces of cocoa wood. One piece, the actual drill, is a slender stick 50 centimeters long. The other piece, of an elongated elliptical shape, with several circular depressions, measures some 15 centimeters in length.

Fire is usually made by two men who alternate rapidly in twirling the drill between the outstretched palms of their hands while a third man holds the elliptical piece with his feet firmly planted on the ground. The hot wood dust emerging from the socket is allowed to flow onto and ignite a tinder cotton, termites' nest, or dry fiber. A lone man can also produce fire by using two sticks of cotton wood or onoto instead of wild cocoa wood. Fire may never be made by women, although they may maintain and use it. Every man owns a fire-drill and carries it with him whenever and wherever he feels it necessary to take his quiver; and that means virtually everywhere, all the time.

The arrow-point quiver itself is made of a bamboo section 45 centimeters long and 10 centimeters wide, whose natural joint serves as the bottom of the container. The top is covered with a dried and molded cover of monkey,

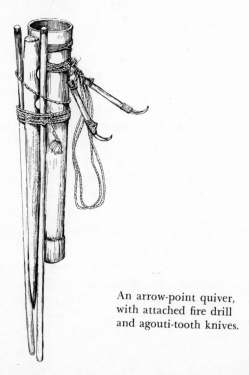

An arrow-point quiver,
with attached fire drill
and agouti-tooth knives.

snake, or jaguar skin. A man carries this quiver on his back, with the aid of a string around his neck. The loop is made of fiber or cotton string fastened around the bamboo section near its top.

The quiver is used to store a variety of arrowheads. One type is a palm-wood point made from a splinter about 25 centimeters long covered with curare poison. Three ring-like grooves are cut into the point, which cause it to break off inside the body of the animal. This palm-wood point is used to hunt monkeys and also as a weapon of war.

A second type of arrowhead is made of a lanceolate piece of bamboo, 3 centimeters wide and 25 centimeters long, sharpened along the edges. It is usually painted red with onoto and decorated with meandering lines. This head is used to hunt jaguars and tapir and is also employed as a weapon of warfare. Lesser game is killed with a smaller variety of the same lanceolate bamboo point.

A third common type of arrowhead is made of a 17-centimeter-long stick of wood provided with a 10-centimeter-long, slender piece of monkey bone, sharpened at both ends. The bone tip is fastened diagonally to the top of the wooden foreshaft by means of fiber and resin adhesive, its upper end serving as the actual arrow point and the lower as a barb. This point is employed mostly for fowling and fishing and sometimes also in battle. According to need, the Yanoama hunter and warrior will select the appropriate arrowhead from his quiver and insert it into a feathered shaft almost 2 meters long.

Arrow shafts are made of so-called arrowgrass, which is in constant demand, and in order to have a large supply available, many Yanoama groups plant whole fields of it. Hunters who come across a stand of wild arrowgrass growing near a river mark the place and come back to collect pieces of roots to replant in their own fields. Bundles of harvested canes are preserved in a dry place under the

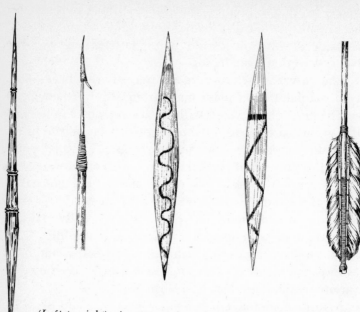

(Left to right): A curare-poisoned arrow point; an arrow point made of an agouti tooth; bamboo arrow points; arrow feathering.

roof, lest they become spoiled by water and humidity. Longer canes are made into hunting arrows; shorter ones are preferred as war arrows. The longer the shaft, the stronger the likelihood that it has some bend or other flaw that would cause an imprecise trajectory. Shorter arrows fly straighter. Feathers of the curassow bird, also known as mutum, are cut in half, and two half-feathers are fastened to the notched base of the shaft by means of resin and cotton thread. The upper end of the shaft is also firmly tied together with cotton thread so that the base end of the arrowhead, or the foreshaft of the monkey-point arrow, has to be forced into the tight cane opening.

A man usually clutches the bow and several arrows in one hand, so as to be ready to shoot at any time. Yanoama men are extremely reluctant to part with their weapons. Even when resting in their hammocks they keep them close at hand. The bow of the Yanoama is most commonly made from a 2-meter-long, smooth piece of pijiguao or peach-palm wood. It has a circular, semicircular, or oval cross-section and is about 2–2.5 centimeters thick in the middle, with both ends tapering down to blunt points. The bowstring is made of twisted vegetable fiber.

No other items of Yanoama material culture could be more specifically identified with the male sex than the bow and arrow. Men take great pride in being good marksmen and respected warriors. Some identify their arrows with an ownership mark, signifying the personal relationship that exists between them and their arrows. An arrow protects its owner and provides food for him and his family. Should it fall into the hands of an enemy, the enemy would have to replace the point with one of his own in order to use it in battle, because an arrowhead never strikes its master.

As a weapon, the bow and arrow may have replaced the club. Even so, clubs are still used to a limited extent by most Yanoama. They are made of the trunk of a small tree or a thick branch and measure about 3 meters in length. The receiving end is sometimes thicker than the handle and covered with knobs. The club is not used in open warfare but, rather, for settling internal grievances between two individuals or between two hostile factions. Personal vendettas can be carried out informally at any time according to the dictates of temper. Group fights follow a formal invitation to the settlement of one of the opposing factions or any other mutually agreeable location between villages. The methods of combat are more or less the same. Two men confront each other with their clubs, and one challenges the other to hit him on the tonsure of his head. The club is grasped with both hands and the blow delivered with full force. If the person struck sustains the blow he will return it, and so on, until one party surrenders. A fallen combatant is helped to his feet by his friends, who spur him on to defend his own honor and theirs. Group duels carried out to restore friendship between feuding groups take place under the pain-depressing influence of epena, a hallucinogenic drug that is inhaled prior to a fight. Nowadays, duels are also carried out by the opponents' pounding each others' chests with the blunt end of an axe.

Before the introduction of metal axes, the Yanoama made hatchets by fastening axe heads of polished black stone to a notched handle with tightly wound strips of vine. The stone axe heads were actually not made by the modern Yanoama themselves; rather, they were and are

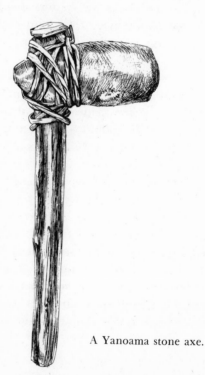

A Yanoama stone axe.

found as ancient objects in their general territory. It is
uncertain whether they were manufactured by their own
ancestors or, as is more probable, by former inhabitants of
a different origin. Today the stone axe heads survive mostly
as ceremonial objects, which play a role in the preparation of hallucinogenic snuff. Two-meter-long spears are
also used occasionally to exact revenge from a group that
is not hostile enough to wage an outright shooting war
with and yet too unfriendly for only a club fight to suffice.

Originally the Yanoama had no boats whatever, and
only recently has the dugout been adopted by some groups.
Both watercraft and paddles lack the perfection of those
manufactured by their Neo-Indian neighbors. Rivers are
generally negotiated on rafts or by wading and swimming.
Ingenious bridges are constructed of crossed poles placed
in the river bed. On these the Indians place other poles
on which they walk, holding onto railings made of lianas
or sticks. Bridges may also be supported by lianas attached
to trees on both sides of the river, on the same principle as
the steel-cable suspension bridge of technological societies.
Occasionally bark troughs are made to drift downstream,
and similar ones are placed in front of the headman's
house each time a feast is held. The ends of the piece of
bark are raised and laced with lianas. For these festive occasions, the trough is filled with boiled plantain soup and
frequented by the hungry celebrants, who help themselves
to the soup with gourd spoons.

One curious negative characteristic should be mentioned here: the Yanoama are among the few indigenous
societies of South America that are altogether lacking in
musical instruments, despite the fact that all of their Neo-
Indian neighbors possess a variety of such instruments.
There is much chanting and singing, both solo and in
chorus, but invariably without instrumental accompaniment.

A permanent Yanoama settlement consists of a circle of huts around an open plaza. The huts stand so close to one another that adjacent roofs overlap, giving the impression of a continuous circular roof interrupted by the diametrically opposed entrances to the settlement. Each individual hut is no more than an oversized windscreen erected on four poles: two in front, 7 meters high; two in back only 1 meter high. The interior side (facing the plaza) is left open. The exterior side is closed with a wall of poles wedged against the roof. The roof itself is made of a thick matting of palm leaves, the stems of which are folded over and fastened to a grate of transverse poles and lianas. Palm fronds are left hanging over the high interior edge of the roof, giving a draped and finished look to the hut and providing protection from the sun. Permanent villages are frequently surrounded by a palisade fence, and during the night the entrances are piled with dry leaves and branches. The only furniture found in a Yanoama house are the hammocks slung in triangular fashion around the fireplace. Provisional shelters have the same triangular shape and consist of three upright poles, 1 meter in length, connected by three 2-meter-long horizontal poles. The flat roof on this miniature shelter is occasionally constructed on a quadrangular ground plan. The Sanemá, to the north, erect oval communal dwellings with pole walls, emulating the Makiritare.

Because of the peaceful symbiotic relationship between the Yanoama and the Makiritare in the Erebato–Ventuari regions, several Neo-Indian culture items have diffused into Yanoama culture. Similar contacts have also been established between the Yanoama and whites. Metal goods are highly desired by all Yanoama, and axes and machetes reached the more remote groups long before personal trading partnerships with whites were established. Those Yanoama villages that are located along rivers frequented

by whites or built near mission stations have functioned
as intermediary traders and have stimulated trading in
general, in some instances even fostering economic spe-
cialization. The Sanemá of the Ventuari concentrate heavily on raising cotton and spinning thread, for which the
Makiritare eagerly trade a variety of goods. Traditionally,
however, each Yanoama group is known as a source of
one or another product of general appeal, for example,
pots, bows, arrowgrass, tobacco, ebena, arrow poison, or
dogs. Trading of these special goods serves as a mechanism
of contact between villages, whose members frequently
visit each other, thereby establishing personal relationships
and commitments.

FOOD-QUEST ACTIVITIES

Until fairly recently, all Yanoama lived as typical foragers of wild vegetables and animal foods. Roaming
through extensive territories, they gathered their sustenance from trees and bushes, the water and the earth. Several centuries ago some took a first tentative step toward
growing some of their own food by replanting saplings of
pijiguao and plantains near their settlements. This practice
soon developed into a regular pattern, leading to system-
atic arboriculture, which afforded the once-nomadic food
gatherers a certain measure of stability, not too different
from that which their Neo-Indian neighbors enjoyed as a
result of root-crop cultivation. Finally, during the past
hundred years, most Yanoama have been gradually adopt-
ing horticulture themselves. However, despite arboriculture and notwithstanding their incipient horticulture, the
Yanoama economy and the activities, rituals, and beliefs
of the food quest bear the traditional imprint of a Paleo-
Indian culture of hunters and gatherers.

The rain-forest habitat of the Yanoama characteristically offers a large variety of wild foods, some in abun-

dance, others in limited quantity. The Indians expend great effort on their gathering activities; still, periods of scarcity are frequent. Palm fruits are quite abundant, and several kinds are eaten—cucurito, seje, corozo, maripa, pijiguao, moriche, and others. However, some of these are found only during a relatively short season, and large quantities have to be collected, because the edible part of most kinds is small, much of the fruit consisting of a tough skin. Some palm fruits cannot be eaten until they have been soaked in water for several days to soften the skin enough to peel.

Climbing the palms to collect the heavy clusters at a height of 20 to 40 meters is men's work, strenuous and dangerous. To collect the fruit of the pijiguao palm, for instance, a man has to climb the spiny trunk with a special device made of poles tied together behind the trunk with a vine, like a pair of scissors. The climber uses two of these devices; he stands on one pair of poles while pushing the second up the tree, then climbs on the upper poles and lifts the bottom ones up.

Heart of palm is greatly relished by the Yanoama and so are Brazil nuts, the shoots of many plants, certain roots, bulbs, and mushrooms. Collected also are several kinds of insects, such as palm larvae, grubs, worms, caterpillars, ants, and termites, as well as rats, lizards, snakes, toads, crabs, and snails. They are eaten raw or cooked. Large spiders are roasted on the embers. Honey is an important source of food, and the Yanoama collect it in great quantities from more than twenty species of bees.

Specialized arboriculture has a great stabilizing effect on the economy of the Yanoama, who, as noted, have cultivated the pijiguao palm and the plantain for centuries. The pijiguao palm also occurs in a wild state in Yanoama territory and is of great importance to many primitive Indian societies in the Amazon basin and in Central America. Before planting the seeds, the women sometimes rub the side with the "eye" on the rock (i.e., the germ pore). It takes as long as six or seven years before a tree bears its first crop, but it will continue to do so for an estimated fifty years thereafter. A fully mature specimen produces upwards of 100 pounds of fruit each year, yielding a large crop at the beginning of February and a much smaller one from June on. This means that pijiguao fruits are usually available for more than six months each year.

The trees are owned individually by the person who planted them, and families are reluctant to move their residence away from a producing pijiguao grove. If they have to leave they will return to their trees periodically to harvest them. But they would sooner cut them down than leave them to be picked by thieves. The main harvest of the pijiguao fruit is the occasion for an important annual ritual, which is the most significant ceremony of the entire Yanoama culture. According to belief, it was the bird Agnacoremasiki that showed the first pijiguao palm to the Indians.

Of unparalleled importance to Yanoama economy is the plantain. Each family strives to maintain a steadily producing garden of plantains and will always try to plant the heavy cuttings in a new field before abandoning an old village site. It takes several years for a plantain garden to mature; the larger the cuttings planted, the shorter the waiting period. When harvesting a bunch of plantains (or bananas), the Yanoama cuts down the entire plant to favor the young suckers which sprout a short distance from the producing tree. In this way, and by transplanting secondary shoots, the Indians hasten the maturing of their grove and thereby achieve greater economic stability.

As mentioned, most of the Yanoama subtribes adopted horticulture in the past hundred years, some earlier, others more recently. Consequently, among some groups it plays a larger economic role than among others. The adoption of horticulture was of course greatly facilitated by the introduction of metal tools, for clearing forest land with stone hatchets and fire alone was a formidable task. Nowadays families rely greatly on the produce of their gardens, with tree fruits (bananas and plantains as well as pijiguao fruit) the staple crops but sweet and bitter yuca (manioc), together with other root crops, such as ocumo, sweet potatoes, and maguey, gaining in importance.

Corn is also becoming important, because it grows fast and because a large quantity of seed can be easily transported to a new garden plot. To speed the growth even further, the women, painting their bodies red for the occasion, soak the kernels in the river, then put them in a basket to germinate in the shade for three days. The germinated kernels are dropped into holes made with a digging stick. There are several food taboos associated with planting of corn; for instance, no one may eat alligator meat lest the roots lack "teeth," and no one may eat the meat of the jabutí tortoise, lest the wind ruin the plants. The Yanoama believe that the leaf-cutting ant taught them how to cultivate corn. Occasionally avocados, papayas, peppers, and cashew trees can also be found in the fields of the Indians.

We have mentioned the nonedible but materially useful crops of onoto, gourds, arrowgrass, and cotton. The Indians also cultivate "magical" plants, especially tobacco and certain other plants used for drugs. Cotton is planted only by men, who maintain that they learned the art from the hummingbird. For digging sticks they use broken bows or any other pointed staff. Two seeds are placed in each hole. A man with a "good hand" grows plants of the desired moderate size, which bear abundant fruit. Both men and women harvest the cotton and season it on banana leaves in the sun. Dried in this fashion, the cotton main-

tains its white color and will not yellow. Magical plants
are used as aphrodisiacs and protective agents, and to
ensure good health. Others are employed in witchcraft to
cause or prevent complications in pregnancy. Tobacco is
greatly appreciated by Yanoama men and women, but for
chewing only, not for smoking. The green or dried leaves
are sprinkled with ashes or earth and rolled into a quid.
This is placed between the gum and lower lip and sucked
for hours. Often a woman prepares the wad for her husband and soaks it in her own mouth before handing it to
him. Men appear to be especially fond of their tobacco
roll and will often share the same wad as a matter of con-
venience as well as friendship. An Indian carries one
most of the time. Sometimes a final quid is shoved into
place after a man's death, to be cremated with him.
The Yanoama believe that it was the bat who first "owned"
tobacco and taught their forefathers how to cultivate it.

The cultivation of tobacco requires great care and special knowledge of planting procedures. The men keep the
tobacco seeds in a bamboo tube. Three days after burning
the felled trees of the garden patch they blow the seeds
over the charred earth and cover them lightly. The young
plants are transplanted and for a week or so they are
protected partially from the sun with large leaves. Then,
if the seedlings look healthy, the protective umbrella is
removed and the tobacco plants are exposed fully to the
sun. The owner of a tobacco patch guards his plot jeal-
ously. Ownership of tobacco plants is highly individual-
istic and reinforced even among members of the same
family. Some owners erect a stick fence around their
tobacco plot to demonstrate their insistence on ownership
rights; sometimes they even implant sharpened bones
to prevent trespassing.

Tobacco seems to be of recent introduction. The
Yanoama say that in former times they chewed the leaves

of the narcotic tala plant in the same way they now use tobacco.

The use of several kinds of hallucinogenic or psychotropic snuff is probably much more ancient. Known among the Yanoama as ebena or epena and elsewhere as yopo or some variant thereof, the snuff powder contains several psychoactive ingredients. The most potent are from a cultivated species of piptadenia (acacia).* Seeds of this tree are roasted, pulverized, and mixed with certain other substances. A less potent snuff is derived from the epidermus of another wild-growing tree. The Indians scrape off the soft layer between trunk and bark and thoroughly knead it into a pliable wad by mixing it with the ashes of various woods and moistening it with saliva. The wad is dried on a potsherd and pulverized with a stone axe. The resultant snuff powder is kept in small calabashes or bamboo containers, which the men carry in their arrow-point quivers. Some carry their ebena wrapped in leaves and hung about the neck.

Trees from which the ingredients of ebena are obtained do not grow everywhere in Yanoama-land; in consequence, there is a trading network involving the much-desired snuff. The hallucinogen may be taken only by men, who by tradition were introduced to it by Omao, the culture hero, himself. Women and children must not even touch the snuff containers unless explicitly told to do so by the men.

To inhale the drug, two men squat opposite each other and insert a small dose into a cane tube, about a meter long, with a hollowed-out and perforated cucurito nut at the receiving end. Each man blows the powder repeatedly into his partner's nostrils until the drug takes effect. The

---

* See R. E. Schultes, "An Overview of Hallucinogens in the Western Hemisphere," in Peter T. Furst, ed., *Flesh of the Gods: The Ritual Use of Hallucinogens,* New York: Praeger, 1972.

trance state is relatively short-lived; the process must be repeated every half hour or so for as long as desired.

The principal traditional reason for taking snuff is to achieve contact with the supernatural—specifically, with animal and plant spirits. Some men appear to undergo rather frightening experiences in the ebena trance, especially if they are young and not yet accustomed to its effects, but others assume expressions of great contentment and can be seen dancing by themselves around the village plaza with arms outstretched or raised over the head. They say that ebena gives them great height and strength, and that they see the environment many times enlarged. Shamans especially use ebena to "ascend" on celestial journeys. The ordinary man may take ebena for the sake of acquiring strength and courage for a duel with clubs or for luck on the hunt, but Shamans take it as an indispensable prerequisite for communication with the Other World, especially for the purpose of divining the nature and cause of illness.

Ebena also serves to protect the hunter from potentially malevolent forest spirits. Carried along on the hunt, the snuff container itself functions as an amulet. Should the voices of bush spirits be heard too close to the village at night, the men will inhale ebena to fortify themselves and thereby avert danger, because the ebena will cause the spirits to leave.

Ebena snuffing appears to be indulged in almost daily by some men and less frequently by others. Recently there seems to have been a shift from ritual to recreational or even escapist use among some Yanoama groups, whose contact with civilization has led to a breakdown in traditional patterns and a surplus of white man's goods with which to barter for scarce ebena ingredients.

Although cultivation of edible and otherwise useful plants has become increasingly more important to the

Yanoama over the past several decades, horticulture cannot as yet be relied upon as a really stable food source.
The gardens are always subject to the usual environmental
hazards. An even more serious threat is posed by Yanoama
groups that have not yet turned to growing their own
food and that are likely to descend on the gardens of their
neighbors to plunder them. The advantages of horticulture can therefore be enjoyed fully only by those with sufficient striking power to protect their fields. The gardens
of weaker villages are at the mercy of raiders who may
force their victims to fall back on the only sources of vegetable foods that never fail: collecting and arboriculture.

With their ever-ready bows and arrows virtually glued
to their right hands, Yanoama men are constantly alert for
game. But, sad to say, game is no longer abundant in their
forest. Even large territories are hunted out in a relatively
short time and are not quickly repopulated. All too often,
hunters return empty-handed from an extended expedition, hoping that in the meantime the womenfolk have
been able to fill the collecting baskets with something to
ease the pangs of hunger. In fact, the men really count on
the women to gather what seems to be an inexhaustible
supply of small creatures, insects, bulbs, roots, and berries.
As long as the women can provide these small edibles, the
hunter's hope for better luck another day is kept alive.
There is a woman's song among the Mahekototeri–
Yanoama that reflects this philosophy and resignation:

> The spider, *waikushihemu,*
> Stood at the door of his house.
> Along came the jaguar who
> Caught and devoured
> Poor *waikushihemu.*

An Indian interpreted the song as follows: Why did the
mighty jaguar, the great hunter of the forest, bother to

catch and eat a tiny spider? Because he was hungry and had nothing else to eat, that's why.

Hunting anything but the smallest creatures is, of course, strictly men's work. At least nowadays, the only weapons used are bow and arrow. Since the bow and arrow are of relatively recent introduction and no Yanoama group has practiced horticulture for more than a century, it seems reasonable to picture their ancestors as nomadic forest foragers who ran their game down and killed it at short range with clubs and spears. Not surprisingly, the Indians are excellent trackers. Should a hunter chance upon fresh tracks, the animal rarely stands a chance. Dogs, the only domesticated animals of the Yanoama, are frequently used to run down larger game. It is not known whether the Yanoama dog was domesticated in pre-bow-and-arrow times; in any event, today it is considered indispensable.

The Yanoama practice two distinct modes of hunting: stalking animals by lone hunters, and communal drives by several men of the village. Hunting drives in which large numbers of men participate for several days are conducted preparatory to a feast. Guests are invited, and the honor of the host village is at stake; besides plantains and other vegetable foods, there must be an ample supply of meat.

Tapir, deer, peccary (wild boar), anteaters, armadilloes, monkeys, paca, agouti, chiguire, crocodiles, lizards, snakes, and turtles are all hunted and eaten. However, members of the cat family—jaguar, puma, ocelot, etc.—are killed for magic reasons rather than the food quest. A tapir pursued by dogs will take refuge in the water, where the dogs hold him at bay until the hunter catches up. To shoot a tapir a Yanoama will select a large lanceolate blade, which tears a considerable wound. If a wounded animal escapes, the blood on its trail makes it easy to follow him.

Peccary are usually hunted in groups, one body of men remaining on the track of the animals, two others working their way from both sides to outflank them. Dogs are generally too noisy for peccary hunts—in fact, if one misbehaves and alarms the boars he may be shot on the spot by his angry master. The men make sure that they approach the wild boars against the wind. Once above the animals, the two flanking groups scare them with sudden noises, causing them to run toward the hunters following on their tracks. Wild boars are preferably shot with poisoned arrows. Successful drives of peccary are said to have netted as many as sixty-seven animals. Sometimes monkeys are also cornered in large numbers and whole bands are killed. No wonder, then, that a particular game area is rapidly depleted, forcing the group to abandon its village and move on. Here again, we see the extent to which the mystique of hunting dominates Yanoama culture: for a Yanoama to be forced to go without meat is tantamount to suffering hunger, and if the choice is between remaining close to a producing garden and migrating to a promising new hunting territory, the latter most often wins out.

Skill and luck are the basic prerequisites for good hunting. The former is acquired through lifelong learning, beginning in early childhood. Young boys practice marksmanship with bows and arrows made to their size. They accompany their elders as soon as they acquire minimal proficiency and are soon capable of skillful tracking, stalking, shooting, and imitating bird and animal calls to bring the prey within range. Hunters communicate with one another by whistling and are reportedly able to transmit messages of considerable complexity in this way.

Success in hunting depends on magic and supernatural powers. It is said that hunters communicate with Omao, a culture hero, or Sohirinariwe, the famous mythological hunter, and other metaphysical beings while out in search of game. Omao is the one who will (or will not) lead an animal toward the hunter's arrow. If no animal appears, the hunter will resign himself to Omao's wish and not question his ill fortune. The entire village would suffer the wrath of Omao should the hunter behave otherwise.

A hunter haunted by bad luck will drain his "dark blood" by stabbing himself in the biceps with a stingray dart and inflicting small cuts on his forearm. Perhaps a menstruating woman touched his weapons or a pregnant woman ate of his game. The hunter may eat only of the meat brought in by his fellow hunters; of his own kill, he may request only the head and a rib bone to keep in a secret spot close to the settlement or in his house. It is with great pride that a man displays these trophies, as evidence of his skill and luck. Only a man with such skill and luck can aspire to maintain a large family and more than one wife.

Fishing plays an insignificant role among the Yanoama. Women fish more often than men. Without efficient tackle, fishing usually amounts to nothing more than picking fish out of a lagoon or rivulet. The women scoop them out of the water with basketry trays, pull them from mud holes in lagoons, or frighten the fish in shallow brooks by shouting and beating the water with branches until they take refuge under stones and rotten leaves on the bottom, where they can be caught with the bare hands. Sometimes the Yanoama employ one or another kind of fish poison (more correctly, drugs) to stupefy the fish, which they then collect by hand as they surface.

Men sometimes shoot fish with small arrows made of slender branches. They watch with interest when the women join in the fun and try their luck at shooting with bow and arrow; otherwise, the bow and arrow are considered proper weapons for males only. Fishhooks are of recent introduction in a few places. In short, among the

Yanoama, fishing, where it exists at all, is nothing more than one of many food-collecting activities, rather than the mainstay of life it represents among such true fishing cultures as the Warao.

In contrast to Neo-Indian horticulturists, the Yanoama prepare no alcoholic beverages. They drink water and juices made of bacabe fruit, the fruit of the moriche palm, bananas, and others.

The work of cooking is customarily divided between the sexes. Women cook bananas, insects, larvae, fruits, toads, birds, fish, and crocodiles. Men cook all the big game and several other foods as well. Insects and spiders are simply roasted on the embers. Larvae are often mixed with ashes, which serve as salt surrogates, or with peppers, before being wrapped in leaves and roasted. Salt is unknown, but a substitute made of the ashes of the karori-heki tree is in great demand. The ashes of a certain plant that grows in waterfalls are also made into an ersatz salt, although tree salt is preferred. Of the water plant, only the leaves are burned to make salt ash. Toads are skinned, cleaned, cooked on the embers, and eaten whole, except for a large bullfrog called wanacoco, whose head must not be eaten. The blood of this creature is also carefully drained because the Yanoama believe it to contain poison; its eggs are considered to be deadly, at least for children. Birds are plucked and fishes gutted before cooking. To cook fish the women wrap them in pishaansi leaves, which are more fire-resistant than banana leaves. Before the first leaves begin to burn the juices stop seeping out and the meal is done.

Meat is barbecued, baked, or boiled. Yanoama men use a four-legged barbecue of wood on which they pile the quartered animals, which are neither skinned nor gutted prior to roasting. All meat must be thoroughly cooked; no Yanoama would eat meat that is the least bit bloody or raw. The entrails are wrapped in leaves and cooked in the hot ashes. On the rare occasions when there is meat left over, the pieces are preserved by smoking them on the barbecue or hanging them from the rafters at a safe distance above the fire.

The Yanoama eat many foods raw—e.g., fruits, palmito, roots, berries, honey, certain larvae, and termites. Geophagy, the practice of eating earth or clay, is prevalent. Both children and adults eat considerable quantities of earth. Adults also eat a white earth that appears to be mixed with the excretion of termites.

There are no regular eating hours. Mealtime finds the women setting the food on green leaves. As a rule the men eat first, followed by the women and children.

SOCIAL ORGANIZATION

The name "Yanoama" does not refer to a nation or a people in the political sense. If we use it here as a generic tribal designation, we do so in order to group together a large number of Indians who inhabit a circumscribed, coherent geographical area, speak closely related dialects or languages, and, despite marked variations, share basically the same technological, socioeconomic, and value systems. But these Indians do not consider themselves as belonging to a Yanoama "nation" and recognize no paramount tribal chief. Even to refer to subtribes like the Sanemá, Waika, and Samatari has little meaning from the Indian's point of view. He considers his village community the largest and most important sociopolitical group he belongs to; and for the village community the Yanoama do recognize a chief.

In fact, village chieftaincy is usually institutionalized among the Yanoama. It is patrilineally inherited from father to son, or passes from elder brother to younger brother. Should no suitable successor be available, the old chief may appoint a capable man who does not belong to any of the dominant village lineages. A young, active, strong son often receives the office from his infirm father.

Some Yanoama chiefs are also leading shamans. In this case, the shaman functions mainly as a peacetime headman, while a man especially experienced in combat leads the village as war chief. The latter office is not hereditary and becomes inactive upon cessation of hostilities. Although the ultimate decision of a major issue, such as moving the village, lies with the village chief, he may, nevertheless, choose to consult with his father, uncles, or brothers before taking action. Old women frequently also achieve high esteem and influence and intervene effectively in the decision-making processes of their village. The chief enjoys considerable prestige, often receives the largest share of spoils, and has the power of command. Even though, generally speaking, polygyny does not constitute a privilege of status and rank, a successful chief stands a better chance of acquiring plural wives than does the common man.

The Yanoama live in a small world whose largest meaningful unit is the village. The founding nucleus of such a village consists of two intermarried pairs of brothers and (consanguineally with them unrelated) sisters and their descendants. The two resulting lineages exchange their women, thereby fostering a web of affinal relationships. As long as the village remains essentially a community of two interrelated exogamous lineages, a chief's authority is largely unchallenged. Even visitors heed his words as long as they stay in the village. However, the political situation becomes more intricate if additional lineages join the village community and intermarry with members of the original pair of lineages. New obligations and loyalties polarize factions and forces too divergent to be kept on a single political course by a village chief.

The strongest obligation a man contracts through mar-

riage is to reciprocate by making a woman of his kin available to the lineage from which he took his wife. These new
affinal (established through marriage) relations tend to
become stronger than the more remote consanguineal agnatic bonds, so that eventually the two interrelated lineages of a plural-lineage village break away to found a new
community. The chief of the old village may continue to
exert influence over this new village also, at least as long
as the nascent group needs the protective power of the
parent village. These ties, however, weaken rapidly. Friction begins to corrode the original amicable feelings, even
though a network of consanguineal relationships exists
between the two villages. When put to the test, loyalties
between brothers and parallel cousins (mother's sister's
children and father's brother's children, who are classified
as siblings) will almost certainly be overridden by those
resulting from the bond of marriage. In fact, friction
among competing patrilineal relatives may trigger the
fission of a village in the first place; resentment and the
desire for revenge are frequently the searing ingredients
in the original matrix of intervillage relations.

The Yanoama distinguish terminologically between paternal and maternal relatives and merge several paternal
relatives (such as father and father's brother) into the
same kinship category, in a process known as bifurcate
merging. The cousin terminology is of the Iroquois type;
matrilateral and patrilateral cross-cousins (mother's brother's children and father's sister's children) are classified
within the same kinship category, whereas siblings and
parallel cousins (mother's sister's children and father's
brother's children) are classed together and distinguished
from cross-cousins. A male calls his female cross-cousin
"wife," whether he is married to her or not, and usually he
will marry a cross-cousin. The Yanoama appear to have
a prescriptive bilateral cross-cousin marriage rule. In a

sense, then, villages are founded on the intermarriage of cross-cousins, and this kinship relationship is possibly the most significant for the individual Yanoama as he goes through his adult life.

Village communities are perpetually on the alert against the not-infrequent raids from neighboring villages, usually in retaliation for suspected sorcery, murders, or food thefts. A raid is considered successful if one or more enemies are killed and the aggressor escapes unrecognized. Duels with clubs are fought between communities to ventilate their hatred and assuage their vengeance in order to avoid entering into a wholesale shooting war. Raids on the unsuspecting enemy are considered proper warfare. Carefully plotted schemes to lure the enemy into a trap or ambush are admired and often lead to a considerable measure of mutual violence. Village communities and individual warriors pride themselves on a reputation for violence, but one sometimes gets the feeling that the acting out of violent behavior for the benefit of an audience is at least as important as the act of aggression itself; certainly, despite a great show of anger and much warlike preparation, raids on another group often result in very few casualties. The warriors prepare themselves for these hostile confrontations by playing a war game in which they shoot at one another with padded arrows. (Games of this sort are also known from the Amazon basin and the Xingú.)

A successful and fearless man will capture women from his enemy to distribute among his younger brothers and friends. A Yanoama warrior will admit that he fights the enemy to capture their women, but one wonders whether this is not frequently a byproduct of Yanoama warfare more than its prime motivation. Captured women are usually gang-raped by their captors. Eventually, however, a woman taken captive on a raid will join the household of one particular man on a free and equal basis. Women, especially old ones, are usually not killed in warfare, but cases are known in which the victors did slay women and children.

LIFE CYCLE AND RELIGIOUS BELIEFS

A woman's menstruation is believed to be a potential danger to the entire community. If a woman fails to refrain from normal activities during her period, the subterranean dwarf spirits will transform her into a rock and destroy the whole village. A menstruating woman paints herself in a special way to alert the village to her condition. Although she need not isolate herself, except during her first menstruation, she will nevertheless keep to herself and observe a number of taboos and restrictions. She must not sit in a hammock, but only on the ground. She may not eat meat, only small fishes and fruit. By no means may she touch men or their belongings. To have sexual intercourse is completely out of the question. She cannot prepare her husband's meals or food for anyone else in the family. For that matter, she must not even touch her husband's bow and arrow lest her contamination render the weapons useless for hunting, in which case they would have to be discarded.

When a woman has passed two or three months without having a menstruation, she informs her husband of her pregnancy, because both parents have to observe a number of food taboos to protect the child in the womb. They abstain from eating certain birds, several kinds of fish, and all big game, lest the life essence of these creatures fall upon the fetus and kill it. The well being of both child and mother is also contingent on the father's protecting himself from chilling rains as he roams through the forest. A pregnant woman may never participate in collecting the bones of a cremated Indian, lest her baby be born feeble and suffer from painful eyes. Both parents and the entire village are especially wary of Siruruwe, a female bush spirit who sometimes becomes angry with mankind when pregnancies occur. Siruruwe announces her dreaded visit by screaming in the forest. Upon entering the village she devours the people, sucking them out so that only their skins remain.

At the onset of labor, the woman goes into the forest near a brook, where she lights a fire and prepares a bed of platanillo leaves. Her mother or sister or the female relatives of her husband accompany the expectant mother. Normally delivery occurs with the mother in a kneeling position. There are usually no complications, but in exceptionally painful cases the suffering mother sends for the shaman, who chants and dances to exorcise the hostile spirits believed to afflict the woman—e.g., the White Monkey, who enters the placenta and holds the baby back by seizing his neck with his prehensile tail, and other spirits that block the birth canal. Immediately after the baby has left the womb, the umbilical cord is severed with a bamboo knife, but no knot is made to tie it off. The mother or helper "cleans" the mouth of the baby with some placental blood on her index finger, so that the child will learn how to speak. The afterbirth is wrapped firmly in leaves and kept under a small elevated windscreen near a big tree. These remains and the screen are burned several months later. After delivery, the mother bathes her baby at the stream by squirting water over him from her mouth. Before being carried into the house, the baby is placed on fresh leaves on the ground, where each witness to the birth steps over him three times to qualify the child for acceptance in the village community. The mother then picks up her child and sits down close to the fire. She abstains from all food and drinks only water during the first day.

The father ignores the arrival of the mother and the child. He reclines motionless in his hammock in a corner of the house, as he did during the actual birth. Among some Yanoama groups he remains in his hammock for ten or fifteen days, since any physical effort on his part would have a grave effect on the baby's health.

On the fifth day, the child's ears are pierced and he receives his personal name. Girls are also deflowered on this occasion by the mother or the grandmother, who repeatedly tears the hymen with the middle finger. Whichever woman gives the first bath to a newborn contracts the obligation to raise it. Crippled babies are almost always killed immediately after birth. Infanticide of girls is also frequently practiced. Male children are much desired, and even a deformed boy may sometimes escape infanticide. The unwanted infant is either thrown against a tree or rock, suffocated by burying, strangled with a vine, choked by stepping with both feet on the ends of a stick placed across its throat, or simply abandoned.

Children are spaced approximately two to three years apart. The mother lactates during this period and refrains from bearing another child in order to sustain an ample supply of milk for the growing breast-child. Intercourse during the lactation period is frowned upon. This practice, coupled with abortion and infanticide, reduces the size of a family considerably, and rarely does one meet a woman with more than three or four children. Abortions are induced by pounding and kicking the abdomen to rupture the amnion.

A Yanoama's personal name is a very intimate possession. He receives it from his father or mother, or else from the chief. No one mentions a person's name in public unless he intends to insult its bearer. For daily communication, the Yanoama use kin terms and address an adult by the name of one of his children; e.g., father of so-and-so (teknonyms). Personal names are usually chosen from the animal and plant kingdoms. Others are simply derived from a particular body feature of the baby or commemorate some special occasion or a circumstance connected with the day of birth. Even a defunct person's name is not uttered lightly. Rather than using a teknonym, one may refer to a dead man by using the name of an appropriate object—e.g., "arrow" for a male—instead of his personal name. Small children's names may be mentioned more liberally but, after they have grown a little, their names are uttered only in their absence and are tabooed. The souls of growing children are always vulnerable to the threat of attack by malevolent shamans of neighboring villages through their magic arrows.

Yanoama parents are very fond of their children. Boys imitate their fathers; girls follow their mothers to learn the chores specific to their sex. But while girls are treated almost like adults from the time they are ten, boys may extend their childhood longer into adolescence. The first menstruation clearly marks a girls transition to womanhood, at which time she becomes eligible for marriage. In fact, she may already have lived for several years in the household of the man to whom she was betrothed as a child.

During her first menstruation a girl is isolated from the rest of the community. She retires behind a tightly woven screen of leaves in a narrow corner of the house and refrains from speaking or making any unnecessary movements. She can leave her cramped quarters only at night, for the purpose of minimal personal hygiene. No man or boy may approach her or even look at her. If an enemy should dare to force the girl out of her hut, he would risk being killed by thunder. Throughout this period the girl has to observe a number of taboos. Girls who speak or weep during their confinement will die. The first day passes in strictest abstinence. On the second day the girl is permitted to suck water from a calabash by means of a bamboo tube.

A Yanoama hunter
bracing his bow.

A Yanoama woman returning
from the field with cooking
bananas.

2

An occasional meal
of small fish cooked
in banana leaves
is always welcome.

3

A Yanoama climbing
the spiny trunk of
the pijiguao palm
by means of a
device made of
poles tied together
like a pair of
scissors.

4

5

A Yanoama blowing psychotropic snuff through the cane tube
of a fellow tribesman.

A Yanoama shaman curing a sick man.

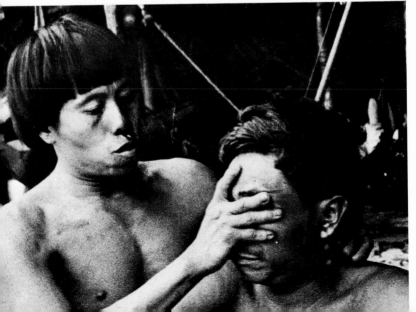

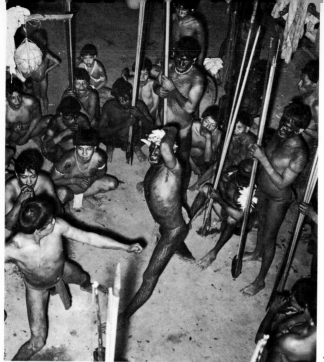

A chest-pounding duel.

A Yanoama consuming the ashes of a cremated tribesman
during an endo-cannibalistic rite.

She would ruin her teeth if she drank directly from the calabash. Only after three days of fasting is she allowed three small bananas, which have been carefully roasted on the embers. Should the bananas be burnt it would signify death for the girl. The confinement period may last from one to four weeks, with the total daily sustenance limited to water and a few bananas, which must be eaten by means of a small stick. The girl must use special sticks to scratch insect bites.

The initiation rite is concluded with a coming-out ceremony in which only the women of the village participate. Very early on this day the pubescent girl's mother ties the branches of the screen together, bathes her daughter in lukewarm water, and paints her body with onoto, without designs. The girl is now permitted to speak in a soft voice but must not look toward the center of the village nor let her glance fall on any male, lest it weaken their legs when they climb the tall palms. Next the branches of the screen are gathered up and burned while the girl is led once around the fire by her mother. Only after the ceremonial burning of the screen is the girl allowed to speak freely.

On the first day of her menstruation she had taken off all her ornaments, strings, and bands. Now she is conducted by the women into the forest to be adorned. While they decorate her, the girl has to stand on a rock, not on the ground, lest she meet an early death. Her long hair is cropped and her tonsure shaven. If facial perforation and piercing of earlobes were not done during childhood, these operations are also performed on this occasion. Adorned and decorated, the young woman leads the procession of women and girls back to the village. They enter by the entrance most distant from the newly initiated woman's house. Slowly the women march across the entire plaza so that everybody can appreciate the girl's beauty. Then for the rest of the day she reposes in her hammock.

Boys pass a less elaborate initiation rite than girls. As soon as the father observes that his son is coming of age, he obliges him to lie down in a hammock for three or four days, during which the boy abstains from eating any food, drinks only water, and remains absolutely silent. On the fourth day, before obtaining permission from his father to go on the hunt, the young man has his tonsure shaven by the shaman and his upper arms scarified. From that day on the young warrior is self-sufficient and independent of his family. He hunts and fights for himself and thoroughly resents anyone's calling him by his personal name.

The male members of a local descent group usually give their women in marriage. As we have noted, this can occur even before the girl comes of age. A child-wife may reside with her husband prior to her initiation, but sexual intercourse is permitted only after the first menstruation. There is no special marriage ceremony; the couple cohabit as soon as the consent of the woman's agnatic kinsmen has been obtained. Should the husband die, the woman will be married to his brother. If there is no brother, the widow may remarry any of her eligible tribesmen about a year after her husband's death.

The Yanoama practice polygyny. A man may be married simultaneously to women who are sisters, but cross-cousin marriages are preferred. Post-nuptial residence is matrilocal; the groom joins the household of the bride's parents and renders them bride-service for some time. But a son-in-law is not supposed to converse or otherwise establish any overtly cordial relationship with his parents-in-law either before or after marriage. Men say that they see a flash of lightning when they look at their mothers-in-law. This avoidance taboo exists also between a woman and her mother-in-law; only an old woman sometimes overcomes her fear and talks to her son's wife.

Yanoama men frequently treat their women harshly,

even cruelly. A woman therefore dreads marrying away from her home village, for then her patrilineal kin cannot protect her from her husband's potential violence. Sometimes the woman's kinsmen are strong enough to keep their sister in residence with them and tolerate her husband's maintaining several wives in different villages. The plural wives of a warrior are often from different villages, where they were obtained more or less violently over a period of several years.

The husband has exclusive sexual rights over his wife, and only with his consent may she have sexual relations with his friends or brothers. Jealousy over women frequently sparks duels, feuds, and even wars. The oldest co-wife orders the younger ones about and retains the right to distribute the food. Quarrels among co-wives are not infrequent, and frustrated women will seek extramarital satisfaction, hoping that their husbands will not find out and physically punish them for this. Homosexuality among women occurs but is considered repulsive. The same is true of incest; it is believed that if a man fails to respect his own sister, his body will not burn when it is cremated after death. Men invite their wives to sexual intercourse in the forest. Children or other adults may not witness the act. Prostitution has not been reported, but female captives are known to be held temporarily in forced group concubinage by the men, both single and married.

Sickness, always of grave concern, is laid to natural or supernatural causes. The shaman is the medicine man and healer. But all adults attempt to heal wounds, set bones, and cure similar injuries, which are usually the result of accident or violence.

Hemorrhages are staunched by rubbing cotton ash in the wound. Wads of cotton are tightly bound over the injury with a strip of bast. White mud rubbed over the entire body of the wounded person is also believed to have

hemostatic properties. The suppuration of a wound is said
to be caused by minuscule animals that eat the flesh from
within, or, in the case of a woman patient, by the harpy
eagle, of whose flesh her father supposedly ate when she
was with child. The open wound is cleansed, then treated
with ebena snuff or the ashes of tarantula skins, which
supposedly cause the tiny animals to run away. The pain
of snakebite is eased by rubbing the wound with tobacco
juice. If a leg has been hurt it is kept tied down and
stretched out.

Broken limbs are set and splinted by women with a
bandage of broken arrow shafts tied closely together. The
patient is confined to his hammock, and the fractured limb
is fastened at an extreme point to a rope hanging from the
roof. The splint is replaced from time to time. Several as-
sistants keep the broken limb stretched while one woman
massages it with hot water. The bast ropes holding the
arrow-shaft bandage in place dry out quickly and have to
be replaced frequently. A healed arm is carried in a sling
for some time and massaged daily with hot water. The
shaman performs curing ceremonies to ease the pain, no
matter what its origin.

Sorcery is considered to be a main cause of death and
disease. Small children especially are the target of enemy
shamans, who send their darts of evil to harm the offspring
of their neighbors. Adults are also targets for the shaman's
magical projectiles, which sometimes even emanate from
practitioners of one's own group. The latter are especially
dangerous, since the unsuspecting healer is unable to detect
them.

Another frequent source of sickness is soul loss. Every
Yanoama possesses a shadow soul (noneshí) in the form
of a small person who resides within his body. This soul
can escape the body and become lost, in which case the
members of the entire community initiate a search. The

men, imitating the behavior and calls of harpies, monkeys, otters, and other animals, run to probe the immediate neighborhood of the village where they suspect the soul might have been mislaid. They also search within the village compound, the plaza, and around the fireplaces. Clutching their babies, women sweep under the hammocks and in the corners of their houses and search on their knees. The fire of the braziers is scattered. If all these activities fail to produce the missing soul, the sick person himself is carried around on the shoulders of some fellow villagers so that he may join in the search. The patient is also placed in a "harpy's nest," built for this purpose with sticks and leaves in the center of the village plaza. Here he is joined by the "harpy eagles" and the "monkeys" and struck on the head with the branches that were used in the search. This facilitates the re-entry of the soul into his body. Those who have participated in the search throw their branches on the "harpy's nest," hoping that they might have picked up the soul of their comrade.

Sickness also comes from a certain class of spirits who attack a person by jumping on his back, making him tremble with fever and fear, and causing nightmares and other psychologically oppressive states of mind. The cure for this kind of sickness lies solely in the hands of the shaman, assisted by his tutelary spirits and, if necessary, by the supreme spirit, Omao, himself.

The tutelary spirits invoked by the shaman with the help of ebena snuff are the "master" spirits of different species and manifestations of nature: birds, fishes, mammals, reptiles, insects, fire, water, stones, solar and lunar beings, the shaman's special tree, and subterranean dwarfs. In short, the shaman invokes spirits from all the cardinal points of the world, from heaven and earth, from all the kingdoms of life and even from minerals and the natural elements. At the shaman's invitation, the "master" spirits congregate in his chest. While one spirit, considered the most pertinent, will be called upon to act as the specific healing agent of a particular illness, all others who are summoned assist according to their abilities. They soothe, cool, and cleanse the suffering person and suck the evil out of his body.

If the situation is grave and the shaman is truly a great practitioner, he may invite such a multitude of tutelary spirits to come and reside in his chest that it may take several marathon seances over a period of several days before they have all entered. This accomplished, he will then proceed to remove them from his own chest, enclosed in an invisible balloon-like container, which he places at a propitious moment on the chest of his patient. The háabalo bird opens a hole in the container, and the particular spirit chosen by the shaman as the specific antidote for the illness diagnosed enters the patient and expels the disease-causing agent. The shaman takes this pathogen between the palms of his hands and flings it into the forest while uttering a resounding roar.

The cure is now complete. The shaman stops taking ebena and breaks his fast by eating small fish. The tutelary spirits disperse, relieving the shaman of the terrific pressure they cause within his body. The more numerous the spirits gathered into his breast, the stronger the pressure. Even the greatest of shamans could not endure it for more than seven days. Nor would this be necessary, for most cases can be cured by calling one or another spirit for help. Yet the shaman is not always successful, particularly when his patient has contracted a white man's disease. Shamans were utterly powerless, for example, when measles swept through a large part of Yanoama-land a few years ago and decimated entire settlements.

All Yanoama men are potential shamans, but only a few of those who receive the supernatural call become truly

great. Prospective shamans undergo prolonged, formal
training by one or several established masters. Training
alone, however, does not suffice. A Great One is he who
has encountered the Great Jaguar, the Daughter of Hikola,
and possibly other supreme spirits while in an ebena trance.
During this encounter the shaman undergoes the classic
shamanic skeletonization process; for example, his flesh is
stripped from his bones and replaced with that of the bat,
the Tobacco Spirit. He may also have his throat and chest
opened and cleaned of blood, and his tongue pulled out
to be replaced with one capable of singing the beautiful
shamanic chants. Women do not receive the gift of shamanism and must never mimic a shaman's songs lest he blow
on their eyes and ears to make them blind and deaf.
Shamans are generally called sablí (shabori), but one class
of curers is also known as kailalá. A kailalá is expert at
extracting pathogens through sucking. The tutelary spirits
of different kinds of fish and the blue-yellow macaw are
their specific helpers. Crab, the alter-ego animal of children, is especially called upon to cure the little ones, and
lizards to help cure women's diseases. But whether sablí or
kailalá, all shamans use ebena snuff to contact the spirit
world. They chant, suck, and massage to cure. In their
malevolent role they can decimate the ranks of the enemy
by blowing magical projectiles which cause sickness and
steal shadow souls.

The sick and dying are, generally speaking, not abandoned, and old people do not seem to be mistreated by the
young. But the physical exigencies of a seminomadic life
catch up with them and become increasingly difficult to
endure. Old women travel on foot, leaning on a piece of
bow. Old men join the women and children on the march
and make themselves useful by carrying some of the utensils and belongings.

Be they old or young, men or women, the dead are all

treated very much the same: the death is lamented, the body cremated, and the residue of ashes ingested by the survivors. Warriors may give expression to their grief by committing suicide, killing someone, or violently dancing about shooting arrows and wielding machetes and clubs. Intimate friends and close relatives wail over the deceased, more quietly deploring his death and urging him to wake up and walk and play as before.

If death occurs in the afternoon, the ritual wailing, chanting, and singing lasts for an entire night; death in the morning sees funeral preparations initiated only a few hours thereafter. The cadaver is flexed to a fetal position and wrapped in a mat of thick sticks. It may also be placed in a large basket. The package is hoisted to the top of a scaffold 2 or 3 meters above the ground, where it is left for several days or even months to decompose. If death was natural, then the híkola of the defunct, his life essence, has left to reside in the body of a close relative to await the cremation of the bones. The soul weighs heavily on the host and must be released as soon as possible. If death occurred from an unnatural cause, such as fever, epidemic, sorcery, or murder, the híkola of the victim invades the murderer and shortly kills him, unless it is promptly released through the cremation of the corpse. The hammock of the deceased is sometimes also deposited on the scaffold. A dead man, as noted, may be provided with a final wad of tobacco, and a child with some plantain or yuca mash to serve as provision for the voyage to the Other World.

Once decomposition has occurred, the skeletal remains are burned and crushed and the ashes are carefully collected into one or several calabashes, baskets, or packages. A portion of the ash is consumed immediately and the remainder on subsequent occasions within a year's time, during a major festival or before the outbreak of a war. Sometimes a slain warrior is cremated soon after he has

died, before his flesh has decomposed. In both cases the
ashes, mixed into a cold banana soup, are ingested by relatives and friends. Cremation of the dead and consumption
of the ashes must occur in some form because otherwise
the híkola could not be preserved as part of the energy
reservoir of the community.

Only if a Yanoama is cremated can his noneshí, or shadow
soul, be propelled to the celestial world of Omao by two
additional animistic principles. The cloud soul, nobolebé,
preserver of a living person's body heat, and the breath
soul, toholilí, reunite with the híkola during cremation.
After death and prior to cremation the nobolebé and
toholilí souls wait in the forest. Stiff and cold, they hope
for an early reunion with the noneshí to carry it in the
smoke of the fire to its eternal destination. They blow the
shadow soul safely past the Moon, who otherwise would
catch and keep it forever in his world of blood. A second
test awaits the ascending soul on the mountain of Omao.
At the foot of the mountain the path divides. One branch
leads to Omao's mansion; the other, to a precipice from
which the soul hurtles down into a lake of fire. (This may
possibly reflect Christian influence.) The souls of all those
who during their life refused to share with their fellow
men are destined for this fiery fate. The souls who enter
into Omao's world enjoy eternal youth and happiness in
celebrating a perpetual festival of pijiguaos.

Omao lives alone in his house and garden, which remain
separated from the abode of the souls by a fence of flowers.
The shaman's trees, which help the practitioners on earth,
are cultivated in the garden of Omao. Shamans who come
to consult with Omao in *hortus conclusus* converse with
him across the fence of flowers. They cannot see him but
may hear his voice. Omao has no parents, only brothers.
In his house, however, he lives in motionless solitude. He
leaves at night so that no one can see him. He uses mes-

sengers to keep him informed of all that happens in the world, and it is they who transmit Omao's orders to all mankind.

BIBLIOGRAPHY

Barandiarán, Daniel de, "Mundo Espiritual y Shamanismo Sanemá," *Antropológica,* No. 15 (1965), 1-28. Caracas.

————,"Agricultura y Recolección entre los Indios Sanemá-Yanoama o el Hacha de Piedra y la Psicología Paleolítica de los Mismos," *Antropológica,* No. 19 (1967), 24-50. Caracas.

Becher, Hans, *Die Suróra und Pakidái: Zwei Yanoami-Stämme in Nordwest-Brasilien.* Mitteilungen aus dem Museum für Völkerkunde, XX. Hamburg: 1960.

Biocca, Ettore, *Los Yanoamas. El último paraíso.* Barcelona: 1967. (English translation, *Yanoáma,* New York: Dutton, 1970.)

Chagnon, Napoleon A., *Yanomamö: The Fierce People: Case Studies in Cultural Anthropology.* New York: Holt, Rinehart & Winston, 1968.

Knobloch, Franz, *Die Aharaibu-Indianer in Nordwest-Brasilien.* Collectanea Instituti Anthropos, I. St. Augustin. Bonn: 1969.

Polykrates, Gottfried, *Wawanaueteri und Pukimapueteri. Zwie Yanoanami-Stämme Nordwest-Brasiliens.* Ethnological Series, XIII. Publications of the National Museum. Copenhagen: 1969.

Steinvorth-Goetz, Inga, *Uriji Jạmi! (Impressiones de Viajes Orinoquenses por Aire, Agua y Tierra.)* Caracas: 1969. (English version by Peter T. Furst, "Uriji Jami! Life and belief of the forest Waica in the Upper Orinoco.")

Wilbert, Johannes, *Indios de la Región Orinoco-Ventuari.* Caracas: Fundación La Salle de Ciencias Naturales, Monografías, No. 8.

Zerries, Otto, *Waika: Die kulturgeschichtliche Stellung der Waika-Indianer des oberen Orinoco im Rahmen der Völkerkunde Südamerikas.* Munich: Klaus Renner Verlag, 1964.

ETHNOGRAPHIC FILMS

1. *The Feast.* Timothy Asch and Napoleon Chagnon. 1967. 23 min. Color with synchronous sound. Copies may be ordered (rental $12.50, purchase $75.00) from Leon Williams, Chief, National Audiovisual Center, National Archives and Records Service, Washington, D.C. 20409.

    Reviewed by Kenneth M. Kensinger, *American Anthropologist,* LXXIII, 2 (April, 1971), 500-502: "The feast is an exciting and (sometimes literally) deadly serious exercise in intratribal, intervillage economics and diplomacy, with both hosts and guests determined to impress others with their ferocity, strength, generosity, and verbal skill. The stakes are high; success results in strengthened, renewed, or newly established alliances under the shadow of perpetual warfare and treachery, while failure may lead to increasing hostility, raids, and death."

2. *Curare.* Barbara Braendli. 1970. 10½ min. Color. Copies may be ordered from the Latin American Center, University of California, Los Angeles, California 90024.

    The film discloses the procedure followed by the Waika, a Yanoama subtribe, in preparing curare, and the taboos observed during the process.

    Copies of films 3-9 may be ordered from Institut für den Wissenschaftlichen Film, 34 Göttingen, Nonnstieg 72, Germany.

3. *Palmfruchtfest.* ("Palm-fruit festival.") Meinhard Schuster. 1954/55. 18½ min. Color.

4. *Feuerbohren.* ("Fire-Drilling.") Meinhard Schuster. 1954. 3 min. Black-and-white.

5. *Herstellung eines Bogens.* ("Making a Bow.") Meinhard Schuster. 1954. 11 min. Black-and-white.

6. *Herstellung einer Hängematte (Baumwolle).* ("Making a Hammock [Cotton].") Meinhard Schuster. 1955. 6½ min. Black-and-white.

7. *Herstellung einer Hängematte und Korbflechten aus Lianen.* ("Making a Hammock and Weaving a Basket from Liana.") Meinhard Schuster. 1955. 7½ min. Black-and-white.

8. *Herstellung eines Pfeiles mit Knochenspitze.* ("Making an Arrow with a Bone Point.") Meinhard Schuster. 1955. 12½ min. Color.

9. *Herstellung einer Pfeilspitze (Bambus).* ("Making an Arrow Point [Bamboo].") Meinhard Schuster. 1954. 4½ min. Black-and-white.

10. *Poisons and Drugs in the Amazon Jungle.* Georg J. Seitz. 1965. 29 min. Color. Copies may be ordered from the Latin American Center, University of California, Los Angeles, California 90024.

    The first part of the film shows the production of a poison for arrows called *mamikorima;* the second part shows the preparation of *parica* by a Tucano shaman who uses the same ingredients as the Yanoama use for their *ebena* but in a different way. The treatment of a patient follows. The third part (about half of the film) shows the production process of *ebena.*

11. *People of the Rain Forest.* Georg J. Seitz. 1960 and 1965. 32 min. Color.

    The film depicts scenes of the daily life of Brazilian Yanoama.

12. *Ebena: Hallucinogenic Ecstasy among the Yanoama.* Inga Steinvorth-Goetz. 1969. 18 min. Color. Copies may be ordered from the Latin American Center, University of California, Los Angeles, California 90024.

    Documents the ritual preparation and use of ebena—hallucinogenic snuff—by Waika men. The drug puts them into a trance in which they feel larger than life and in possession of great physical strength. Most important, the drug enables them to enter into communication with the *hikola,* the spirits of animals and plants, whose voices and counsel they perceive while in the trance.

3 The Fishermen: The Warao of the Orinoco Delta

The Paleo-Indian way of life underwent drastic changes when the large Pleistocene mammals became extinct, some 7,000 years ago. The big-game hunters were now limited to smaller prey, unless they turned to the coast, the rivers, and the lakes. The life of many Paleo-Indian hunters shifted to that of Meso-Indian fishermen. By 7,000 B.P., Indians throughout Venezuela, and especially along the coast, were caught up in this transition, and during the following 4,000 years—until 3,000 years ago—they adjusted to their new way of life. In the interior, small-game hunting continued, and much more importance was attached to the collecting of fruits and wild plants and to river and lake fishing. Some populations developed incipient horticulture toward the end of the Meso-Indian period, and Venezuelan Indian life experienced a vigorous development comparable to the complexity of early Amerindian life elsewhere in the New World. Groups probably became geographically more restricted. Tools now included the bow and arrow, bone spatulas, stemmed stone projectile points, bone points, bipointed stones that were possibly hurled in slings, and, characteristically, a shell adze, the so-called gubia, made from a conch shell. This gouging tool is of great utility in making dugout canoes from tree trunks. It was probably used for that purpose during the Meso-Indian period, and boats were developed that enabled the Venezuelan Indians to carry their culture to the islands of the Caribbean. Pottery was also made by some Meso-Indian horticulturists.

Today the Meso-Indian type of fishing culture survives among the Warao of the Orinoco Delta. Among the other Meso-Indian-type fishing cultures of Venezuela are the Paraujano of the Laguna de Sinamaica. Some of their culture traits resemble those of the Warao, but linguistically and genetically the tribes are not closely related. The Warao share several culture traits with the Yanoama, to whom they appear to be linguistically and genetically related.

The generic name of the Warao tribe means "Boat People," and it is possible that the boat became their most notable possession at a time when the dugout was first developed by some Meso-Indian tribes. Nonmetal adzes are a common Warao artifact. Fish and seafood form part of the "true food" for human beings, hunting is of little importance, and horticulture is a recent introduction. Exploitation of the moriche palm has great economic significance.

The majority of the Warao inhabit the labyrinthine swamps and waterways of the Orinoco Delta in eastern Venezuela. Smaller groups live to the west of the delta, in the neighboring states of Sucre and Monagas; still others are found southeast of the main distribution area, along the swampy coastal belt of Guyana and Surinam. The Warao homeland comprises some 17,000 square kilometers, between 8° and 10° North latitude and between 59° and 62° West longitude. They have lived in this region since prehistoric times, protected by their difficult environment from Afro-Europeans and other Indian tribes, none of whom succeeded in conquering their stronghold.

The first missionaries, venturing into the delta in 1925,

met only a few Creoles. Small groups of Arawak, Carib, and possibly some Indians of other language groups appear to have penetrated the peripheral delta areas, but these either disappeared or were absorbed by the Warao and are therefore difficult to trace. In short, the Warao are one of the few Meso-Indian peoples of South America still surviving as a substantial and thriving tribal society, relatively free of genetic or cultural admixture.

The 1960 National Census for Venezuela registers 11,412 Warao (Guaraúnos) settled in some 249 villages. However, largely because of improved medical care, the Warao population is rapidly increasing. Counting the 500 or so Warao living in Guyana and Surinam, the total should now be about 14,000.

THE HABITAT

The delta region of the Orinoco is a fan of alluvial deposits accumulated during the relatively recent geological epochs of the Quaternary. Bounded on the south by the Orinoco River proper and on the west by the Manamo, this area is splintered by innumerable rivers into a multitude of islands of varying size. The average mean temperature is 26° C, the humidity 60 to 80 per cent. There is a rainy season, which lasts roughly from July to September, and a dry season from October to June, with annual precipitation ranging from 100 to 200 centimeters.

Hot pluvial forests cover the islands of the Orinoco Delta. In the Upper Delta, large portions of the gallery forest have been cleared for agriculture by the predominantly Creole population. Trumpetwood, silk-cotton, and guamo trees are much in evidence; shady bucares are the only remaining vestige of the coffee and cacao plantations that flourished in colonial times. In the Intermediate Delta region, a patchwork of small channels and semi-inundated islands, the flora is less uniform. The banks of wide rivers

are lined with asymmetrical forest galleries. Twisted trees
30 meters high, smothered with lianas, flank the river bank
that sustains the main current. Timiche, manaque, and
cubaro palms struggle through the dense mat of air plants
(epiphytes). On the opposite side, where the water flows
more slowly, tall palms and other trees shoot up from behind a barrier of araceae. Manaque, manaca, and algarroba
are among the giants. Air plants are less conspicuous on
these trees, but become more abundant along the banks of
smaller waterways with little or no current. Here they grow
like cobwebs, shrouding the thick palms and other trees
lining both banks. Timiche, manaque, castañon, rubber,
guamo, and orchid trees are common. Floating islands of
water plants drift back and forth with the tide, which
periodically inundates the Intermediate Delta region, favor-
ing the abundant growth of palm trees such as the manaca
and moriche. Interspersed among them are the tall, slender
trees of the Leguminosae or pea family. The timiche palm,
however, prefers somewhat higher ground away from the
tidal flood. Mangroves appear sporadically inland but completely dominate the coastal belt.

In pre-agricultural times the actual habitat of the Warao
was the palm-rich region of the Intermediate Delta and the
coastal mangrove swamps. This seems hardly more than a
marginal niche at best; that they were able to make it completely viable is certainly an admirable cultural achievement. Maximum exploitation of the available flora, together with utilization of abundant fish and bird resources,
guaranteed a relatively stable year-round diet on which the
Indians could rely to the almost total exclusion of the
equally abundant and rather uniform mammalian fauna of
the delta. One result of acculturation has been the hunting
of animals, but this is still restricted to a few species of
game. It is interesting that some of the nutritionally most

valuable game animals, especially tapir, and here and there also deer and paca, are traditionally tabooed; in addition, such riverine mammals as the nutria and fresh-water dolphin are also considered forbidden meat. According to the Warao, such animals "have blood very much like people"; eating them would be almost akin to cannibalism. However, birds have been hunted since the mythological "first times."

LANGUAGE

Considering the vast distribution area of the Warao and their division into hundreds of small groups, one might expect considerable linguistic diversity. But this is not the case. All Warao speak one and the same language, which, until recently, was considered to be "independent"—that is, unrelated to any other South American language. This classification was challenged some years ago by linguists who discovered a distant relationship between Waraoan and Chibchan. Languages of the Chibchan family are spoken mainly in northwestern South America and southern Central America, so that the identification of Chibchan affiliation provides a link between the Warao and the tribes to the west. As we saw, Yanoaman is also supposed to be of Chibchan affiliation. In addition, a distant relationship exists between Yanoaman and Waraoan, and—less certainly—the latter may even be related to the Ye (Gê) of eastern Brazil.

Not surprisingly, the Warao practice no form of writing. Their numerical system is vigesimal (based on the number twenty): five is the outstretched hand, ten is all the fingers, and twenty is all twenty digits of a man—that is, of a Warao. Thus the name "Warao," although derived from *wa* = boat and (a) *rao* = people ("boat people"), can also be employed to designate the number twenty.

MATERIAL CULTURE AND TECHNOLOGY

Travelers passing through Warao territory at the beginning of the nineteenth century reported the native dress
of these Indians as "scant," consisting of little more than
a "belt." This was probably a traditional cotton string
worn plain or adorned with pendant shells. In more recent
times Warao men adopted a breechclout made of manaca
fiber, replaced by one of cloth when the Warao came into
sustained contact with Creole populations. Women also
used a fiber loincloth, and in some of the more remote
regions of the delta they continue to do so even today.
Nowadays a man wears trousers, a shirt, a belt, and a hat
like his Creole neighbor. The women wear handmade,
ankle-length sleeveless dresses, hanging straight from one
or both shoulders. These were introduced in the peripheral
delta even before the arrival of the missionaries, as indi-
cated by their Caribbean island name—"nawa." Children

A Warao woman's
necklace of seeds.

run naked about the villages until they are eight or ten
years of age.

Necklaces of red, blue, and white glass beads are worn
in thick ropes by the women. In some areas narrow red-
bead necklets are also seen on the men. Originally necklaces were made of shells, seeds, bone, and teeth. These,
and even the necklaces fashioned of glass beads, are still referred to as do-a-i, "neck's teeth."

The Warao produce a variety of wicker and checker
basketry, mostly made of strands prepared from a reed-like
plant called itiriti. Weaving techniques vary from piece to
piece but generally resemble the work of the tropical-forest
Neo-Indians, from whom basket weaving as such was probably adopted. The Warao themselves say: in the beginning
the Warao were very ignorant—they had to fell the moriche
with hand axes. But then they conquered a neighboring

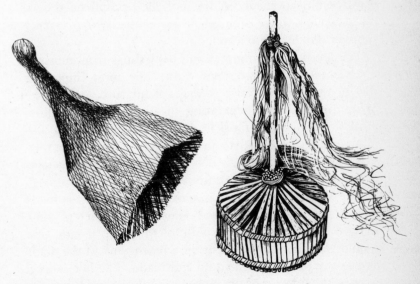

Typical Warao basketry hats. The one shown at the left is made of
the fiber container of timiche-palm fruits. The other is a ceremonial
hat made of the leaf stalk of a moriche palm.

tribe of cannibalistic Indians, from whom they learned the technique of basketry and also how to fashion hoes and other implements. Warao basket weaving is restricted mainly to the making of fire fans and various kinds of baskets; woven mats are rare and, properly speaking, neither the portable fish weirs nor the triangular sails made of moriche-leaf stalk come under the category of basketry. Both men and women make baskets, but the ingenious yuca press, which works somewhat on the principle of the Chinese basketwork "finger puzzle" and which the Warao adopted from tropical-forest Indian neighbors, is usually manufactured by men. Most Warao basketry has the original brownish color of the natural material employed, but some artisans produce very decorative pieces with patterned light and dark strands. Aboriginal Warao containers still in use today are calabashes, wrappings of palm leaf, and tray-like objects made of dry moriche or timiche shoots. To scoop up water or moriche juice, the Warao usually simply roll a leaf into a cone.

The netting of hammocks and baby slings from moriche fiber is exclusively women's work. The most important raw material for Warao cordage of all sorts is moriche fiber, the epidermis separating the unopened accordion-pleated folds of the moriche leaf. Moriche string is also interwoven with itiriti to produce very durable trumpet-shaped carrying baskets, which the women tote with shoulder straps rather than a tumpline.

The Warao hoe, a most important implement, is made of a blade of moriche wood some 75 centimeters long, wedged into a cleft in a handle of the same length, and bound with moriche string at the working end of the blade and at the junction of handle and blade. The hoe is used to chop the interior of the moriche trunk to the consistency of sawdust for the making of yuruma starch.

Ever since they first saw metal tools, the Warao have

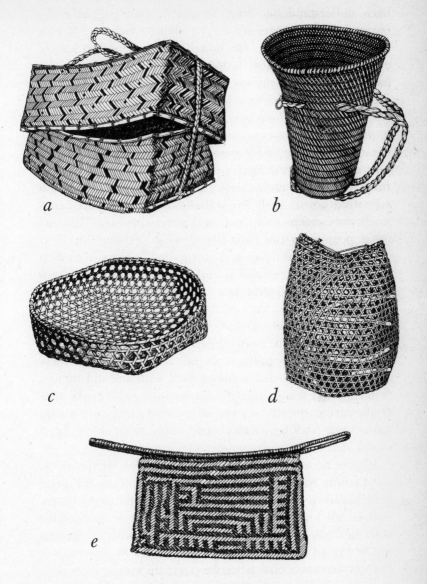

Warao basketry used as a container (*a* and *b*),
a tray (*c*), a bird cage (*d*) and a fire fan (*e*).

been understandably eager to obtain axes and adzes by barter, because they make the manufacture of dugout canoes so much easier. The metal adze now used to hollow out large trees for boat building probably had its aboriginal forerunner in the so-called gubia, an adze made from the innermost whorls of a large conch.

Certainly no single item of Warao material culture is more vitally important than the dugout. Without it human life in this swampy refuge would be inconceivable. On long expeditions the boat, propelled by paddles and sometimes with a triangular sail of moriche-leaf stalk, serves as a floating house. In it the Indians travel, transport heavy loads, fish, sleep, cook, eat, and play; they are "Warao" (boat people) in the most literal sense. Famous for their skill in canoe building and navigation since the earliest days of the discovery and Conquest, the Warao have been sought after as shipwrights and navigators by explorers of many nationalities. Very likely the Indians made dugouts even in remote prehistoric times, felling cachicamo or sassafras trees with the help of fire and hollowing them out by burning and chopping with the shell gubia. The widening of the hull is still accomplished with the aid of fire. A man often teams up with his sons-in-law to make new boats during the dry season; in ancient times, when iron tools were lacking, such cooperation must have been essential.

Expert boat builders enjoy great prestige in the tribe, for reasons that go beyond simple admiration for good craftsmanship into the realm of the supernatural. An expert canoe maker is one who has learned to perfect his skill through an encounter (in dreams) with a Serpent Spirit, who is reputed to have served the Warao culture hero Haburi as a boat when he made his escape from danger. The honor of having been chosen by this Serpent Spirit extends beyond the present life, for such a man will go forth after death to continue his existence in her presence.

Unlike the Yanoama, the Warao employ a variety of musical instruments, largely as accompaniment for various rituals. There is religious song and secular song, the latter usually performed without instrumental accompaniment. The use of musical instruments is restricted to men, underscoring their primary role in religious ritual as well as the ritual nature of the instruments themselves.

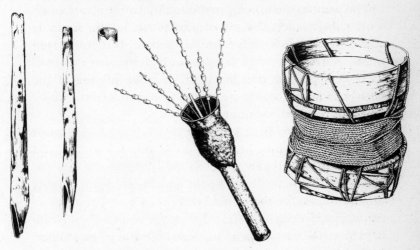

Musical instruments used by the Warao: wooden flutes; a ceremonial single-reed instrument *(after Roth)*; and a drum.

Among the wind instruments, flutes of wood as well as bone have been seen. The wooden flute is a reed tube; the bone flute is made from the tibia of a deer; both have only three stops. Deer-bone flutes are often played by young lovers, whose music may be considered magical. Simple whistles are made of crab claws and of the shell of a large snail. By cutting the apex off a large conch—usually the Caribbean *Strombus gigas L.,* or Queen Conch—the Warao fashion a fairly sonorous trumpet, which is used as an instrument to turn away death or signal victory, success in a fishing expedition, and the like.

A peculiar single-reed instrument, the so-called isimoi, is made from a piece of moriche stalk with a small calabash glued to one end to serve as resonance chamber. This is an exclusive cult instrument blown by the "master of the isimoi" during the annual yuruma festival; its ritual nature and cultic use relates the Warao to many other South American tribes possessing sacred wind instruments.

The tambor-drum, of post-Columbian origin, is beaten with a single stick as the villagers set out for the moriche groves to collect starch for the cult festival. It is also played in the festival itself, by a man leading the procession of participants to the dancing platform. The playing of the deer-bone flute is also an integral part of this festival, which has deep religious meaning.

Strings of dried fruit hulls are tied to the tops of staves to serve the clarinet player as accompanying rattlesticks. Similar rattlestrings are worn on the ankles of the dancers, whose feet rhythmically stamp the dancing platform. Highly important also are the sacred rattles used by religious practitioners for curing as well as during the cult festival. Holding the sacred rattle upright before him, the priest-shaman flies to the zenith of the firmament and from there to the Ends of the World, where he visits Supreme Beings. Small calabash rattles are used by the men during a fertility dance, and basketry rattles may once have served a similar purpose.

Some Warao are quite adept at the violin, an adopted instrument they have been making for several centuries. Recently portable phonographs have found their way into a few houses in the delta, and in the night they blare out the same few scratchy discs *ad nauseam*. Simultaneously with these machines came the Western practice of dancing in pairs, with the partners facing each other. This mode is

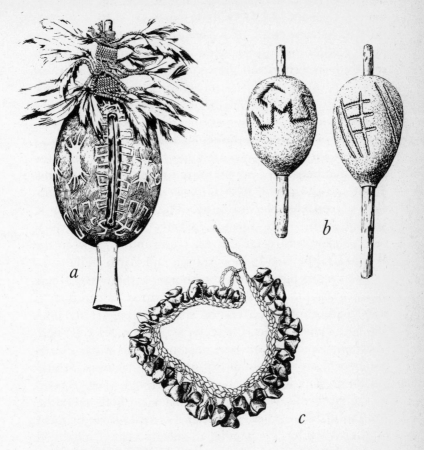

A shaman's rattle (*a*); small calabash rattles used during the fertility dance (*b*); a rattle string of fruit-hulls (*c*).

completely alien to Warao tradition, where lines of men and women moved rhythmically back and forth from one another, or in a circle. Aboriginally, dancing, like instrumental music, appears to have had an exclusively religious function.

Strip the Warao material culture of all tools and imple-

ments of recent introduction, and surprisingly little remains. All metal objects would disappear: there would be
no knives, axes, adzes, or machetes, no fishhooks, cooking
pots, needles, or scissors. Almost everywhere in the delta
the younger generation grew up accustomed to all these
tools, but thirty or forty years ago such things were scarce
or unheard-of. Pottery has never been known among the
Warao, and neither has weaving. Until a few years ago,
only the primitive forerunner of the hammock, made of
two moriche-leaf fans knotted together, was in use; the
netted hammock is a recent introduction. Except for the
drum and the violin, most musical instruments are probably of considerable antiquity. The boat, too, is quite
ancient, and so are various basketry techniques, which
reach back at least as far as the first encounters between the
Warao and the Neo-Indian Arawak and Carib Indians.

The rectangular, saddle-roof house without walls may
also predate the Conquest by two or three centuries. It is
still in use, but nowadays the stilt dwelling set on piles
1½ to 2 meters above the water or swamp level is more
common. However, in some regions of the delta, houses
are erected on a horizontal substructure that rests directly
on the ground. Villages are usually located where a bend
in the river affords an unobstructed view both upstream
and downstream. These settlements consist of one or more
lines of dwellings set parallel to the riverbank, inhabited
by several nuclear families or one or more extended families. Accordingly, the houses may range in size from 4- by
5-meter huts to more imposing dwellings several times as
large. The approximate over-all height is 4.5 meters. A
settlement may consist of only one or two houses or as
many as ten and even more. According to the 1960 census,
however, based on 249 settlements, the average village is
small, sheltering only about 50 persons.

Each village has certain structures set apart for specific

purposes. At one end of the rectangular ground plan of a settlement is the menstruation hut, where women seclude themselves for the length of their period. These may be small 4- by 5-meter houses with four walls or only simple windscreens. The kitchen house and grain barns are of roughly the same size.

A primitive temple, or shrine, stands at the opposite end of the village from the menstruation hut. It is somewhat taller than the usual living structures. The lower floor is reserved for the barrel-like container in which moriche flour is stored during the annual moriche festival. On the upper floor are the wooden boxes or box-shaped baskets that contain the sacred stone, various wooden

The sanctuary as it appears during the moriche festival, with the walls of the lower compartment cut away to show the container filled with the offering of yuruma starch.

images, rattles, and other sacred paraphernalia belonging
to the priest-shaman. Access to the upper level is provided
by one or two poles leaning against the platform of the
second floor. The temple is closed on all sides by screens
of tightly arranged or else loosely hanging timiche leaves.
Between village and temple there is a dancing platform
constructed by manaca beams or strips of moriche bark
laid in juxtaposition across a frame of manaca.

The occupants of a dwelling sling their hammocks next
to one another in family groups. A woman keeps a fire
nightly under the hammocks of her family to ward off the
cold, as well as mosquitoes and possibly a stray jaguar.
Utensils and other equipment belonging to each family
are kept in baskets hanging from the house beams or
tucked into the thatch of the roof. Basket "boxes" and
covered baskets are also used and stored away on the beams
of the roof structure.

FOOD-QUEST ACTIVITIES

The gathering and collecting of wild foods have traditionally played a very important role in Warao economy.
Formerly, both men and women were constantly on the
lookout for a wide variety of edibles, and their children
were trained from an early age to be similarly alert to
nature's bounty. With agricultural products increasingly
available, there is less attention now to the quest for wild
foods. Nevertheless, the Warao still diligently collect fruits,
palm cabbage, moriche starch, wild pineapple, honey, and
herbs. They gather larvae, snails, crabs, and the eggs of
turtles and iguana. Fruits are usually collected by the
women after the men have felled a tree, for rarely does one
happen on ripe fruits that have fallen to the ground.

The Warao are keen observers of their environment.
Long boat trips provide the chance to mark the object of
a future quest, and they avidly watch the forest galleries

on both sides of the river, pointing out various items of interest such as stands of moriche, timiche, manaca, seje, purgua, or other trees whose fruits they eat and whose by-products are of importance. They also watch the river banks for certain plants and shrubs whose shoots provide refreshment on long expeditions. The delta Warao especially enjoy the acid taste of Caña de la India, which grows around the lagoons. Quantities of merey trees are planted for their fruit next to lemon and orange trees in garden plots around the houses of the Guyana Warao. A refreshing drink can be prepared from the fruit stems of this plant, and the seeds may be roasted. Wild pineapples are collected in January, and the Warao remember the bygone days when this sometimes led to hostile encounters with Carib Indians, who invaded their territory precisely to collect this highly relished fruit.

For the pre-agricultural Warao, the starchy pith (yuruma) of the moriche palm provided a major source of nourishment during much of the year. Even today, when many Warao practice at least some horticulture, yuruma continues to be an important staple for many local groups. There is no doubt that the discovery of the techniques of processing moriche pith into an edible substance spelled the difference between survival and starvation in the newly occupied swampy delta—it, above any other source of food, turned this normally inhospitable environment into a viable niche. In view of its many uses, to call the moriche the "tree of life" of the Warao is more than a mere figure of speech. The blessing represented by its starch is clearly recognized by the Indians themselves, for they refer to it, especially in combination with the morocoto fish, as the "true food" of man. More than a vital source of human sustenance, it became elevated to a position of great ritual significance, as a medium of communion between men and the deified kanobos (spirits). It is still collected and proc-

essed, not only as a staff of life, but as a sacrificial offering
to communicate with the supernatural; the religious festival connected with the main yuruma harvest is the high-
light of the Warao year.

Did the Warao "discover" the edible moriche pith, or
was it a case of cultural borrowing? Warao oral tradition
tells us that they were not themselves the "inventors" but
adopted yuruma, together with the appropriate implements, from other people. This does sound historical, but
so far we have no concrete evidence that early South American Indians exploited the moriche for anything other than
its fruit (as the pre-agricultural Yanoama do to the present day), or that yuruma was adopted as a principle staple
by anyone other than the Warao themselves. It may well
be that the contemporary technique used by the Warao to
turn the starchy pith of the moriche into an important
source of nourishment represents the survival of a formerly
more common tradition, reaching back into the remote
prehistoric past and perhaps predating the first entry of the
Warao into the delta. This might explain why the ancestral
Warao were evidently not afraid to settle permanently in
so difficult a terrain; whatever else the delta might have
lacked in resources familiar to the Indians, at least it was
rich in moriche. In any event, for the Warao this form of
unspecialized arboriculture provided a measure of economic stability like that of the Yanoama based on the
pijiguao and plantain palms and not unlike that achieved
by others through horticulture.

In addition to its numerous other uses, the moriche also
provides the Warao with their favorite grub, the fat white
larva of a beetle which seem to specialize on the pith of
this palm. Many kinds of beetle, bee, and wasp larvae are
collected, but those found in great numbers in decaying
moriche palm trunks are especially valued. Honey is another favorite; entire families and even villages join to-

gether on honey-gathering expeditions. Tree beehives are
felled and the insects smoked out. Everyone drinks his fill
of honey mascerated with water. What is left is collected
in provisional receptacles of manaca bark or calabash or
bottle gourds and carried home for later consumption. The
Warao do not consume honey in its undiluted form. Beeswax is carefully preserved for various purposes.

Traditionally, most Warao shun chicken eggs and also
the eggs of any wild bird, but this is changing under Creole
influence. In contrast to birds' eggs, the eggs of turtles and
iguanas are much sought after; very likely these have been
part of the regular diet since time immemorial. Various
rivers in the delta are known as "cooking place for snails,"
because of the abundance of an edible species of large
black-shelled snails along their banks.

It is with special excitement that the Warao look for-
ward to the crab season in July and August, when spring
tides force the crabs closer to shore and up onto the mangrove beaches. In the past whole villages would take to
their canoes and move to temporary camps near the coast.
Some still do so, but now that outboard motors are becoming common in the delta, greatly speeding up communica-
tions, the Indians often leave their permanent settlements
only for shorter, one- or two-day crab-catching excursions,
passing the night in their canoes and returning home the
following day with their mapire baskets full of delicious
crabs. Chiefly these are of the common yellowish-brown
variety, about the size of a man's hand, but a somewhat
larger and less common blue variety is also relished. Catch-
ing crabs is man's work. The mangrove swamps are full of
mosquitoes, and to protect themselves the men smear their
bodies with mud. There are crabs by the thousands, and a
catch of 75 to 100 crabs per man in an hour is not unusual.
So impatient are the collectors for the delicate taste of the
meat that they often crack open the crabs on the spot and

suck out their contents raw. When the baskets are filled and the canoes head home, the great conch-shell trumpets are sounded to announce the success of the hunt and the imminent return of the menfolk. There are great feasts then; some of the crabs are eaten raw but more commonly they are boiled until their shells turn red and the flesh inside a delicate white, with the exquisite flavor so appreciated the world over.

Not too long ago, fish and seafood were the most important source of protein for the Warao, who are a fishing society *par excellence*. But here again there are taboos: just as certain land mammals are not eaten, so certain aquatic animals and fish are taboo because of magical properties—for example, several species of catfish, cachama, pallara, and guitarillo. The fish most frequently caught include the morocoto, nontaboo species of catfish, guabina, aguadulce, laulau, buco, coporo, zapoara, guaraguara, and arenque.

The Warao employ a number of fish-catching methods. In areas south of the Orinoco they go after the guaraguara with their bare hands, digging them from their holes in the river banks at low tide. They fish small pools by first filling them with mud, after which they can pick out the fish by hand or take them with a cudgel or machete or in dish-like baskets. The shallow waters of lagoons are dragged with conical baskets, or fish may be scooped from the water with baskets tied to poles. Despite the rudimentary nature of these techniques, the fishermen enjoy considerable success and often return from their excursions with many small fish strung on a vine. The gorge, a hunting device of respectable antiquity, was adapted by the Warao first to catch larger varieties of fish; nowadays a modified "gorge," consisting of a fat larva tied to a flexible pole, is still used to catch the small hoko fish, which is flipped into a basket when it grabs and swallows the bait. Today, however,

1   The family corner in the pile dwelling of the Warao.

2   Basket-weaving is an incessant
    occupation among the Warao.

A Warao woman netting a   3
hammock of moriche string.

4   A Warao harpooning a morocoto fish from a boat.

5 Warao women collecting the excavated pith of a moriche palm.

The pith of the moriche is placed in a basketry sieve on a stand and triturated with water. The starchy yuruma collects in the receptacle below.

6

7

The Warao shaman makes use of a sacred rattle in curing.

A truncated unfinished dugout, tightly secured with palm leaves and lianas, serves as a coffin. A layer of mud is placed on top to trap the spirit of the deceased.

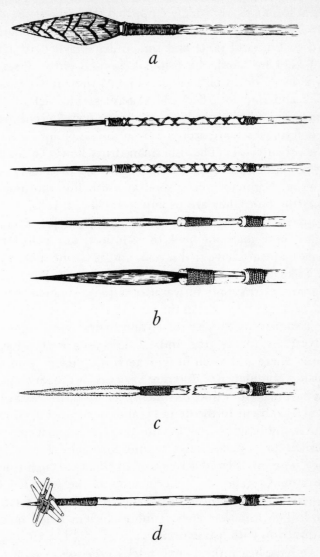

Various types of arrowheads in use among the Warao:
(*a*) a wooden-headed arrow; (*b*) arrows with palm-wood
heads; (*c*) an arrow with a head made of sting-ray spike;
(*d*) a "bird" arrow.

metal fishhooks are widely employed throughout the delta
and have largely replaced the traditional gorge. Sometimes
tied to line and pole, and sometimes attached to a float
and held by hand, the fishhook is used either from the
river bank or from a canoe. The Warao of Guyana tie
hook and line to a float of calabashes. The delta Warao
sometimes use moriche-leaf-stalk floats about 75 centimeters
in length, which are dropped from the canoe into the river
at short intervals. The fisherman drifts slowly in his boat
along ten or twelve such floats. These are extremely sensi-
tive and begin to bob as soon as a fish hits the line and
takes the bait; they are promptly retrieved, rebaited, and
dropped back into the river. Sometimes a fisherman at-
taches more than one hook to each float, just as in former
times he would have tied several gorges to one float. Chain
hooks have also been observed in recent years. For bait the
Warao seek a supply of wahuba, a 15-centimeter-long eel-
like creature that lives in the mud of river banks. Small fish
are also used as bait, as are certain fruits.

Needless to say, the Indians are very well informed
about where and when in their territory they may find the
greatest abundance of different varieties of fish. Such places
are havested from time to time by means of fish weirs (fish
dams are absent in the delta because of the lack of stones).
The portable weirs used for this purpose are mats made of
moriche or timiche stalks bound together with moriche
fiber. They are placed across a small stream at high tide; as
the waters recede, the fishermen spear the stranded fish,
toss them ashore, or simply wade in and grab them by
hand. The fish weir is even more efficient when used in
conjunction with fish poisons.

We have heard the Warao refer to the use of lights and
machetes for fishing at night, a technique used by their
Arawakan and Cariban neighbors. Fully automatic fish
traps, however, as they occur among neighboring tribes in

Guyana, are atypical for the Warao and are completely
lacking in the delta.

In use throughout the delta are the fish spear, multipronged arrow, harpoon arrow, and harpoon. Spears made
of macanilla are used chiefly to kill and collect fish which
have been trapped or poisoned in weirs. The Indians use
multipronged arrows or harpoon arrows to shoot fish lured
near the boat or shoreline by tossing the appropriate bait
into the water. Much more important than spear and arrow,
however, is the harpoon. The Indians dangle a bait of the
rabano plant over the surface of the water close to the
"tracks" (ripples on the water) of the morocoto and harpoon it as it breaks surface. The harpoon has a shaft of

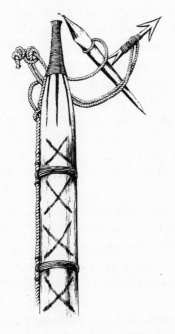

A Warao harpoon (*left*) and a trident
arrow (*right*), used for fishing.

moriche-leaf stalk some 2 meters in length, with an iron point that sits on a short, wooden, movable toggle attached to both shaft and point by string.

The various fishing methods employed by the Warao appear to be more efficient on the smaller rivers and lagoons of the Intermediate Delta region than for fishing the wide rivers of the Upper Delta. Hooks are a relatively recent introduction among the Warao (especially chain hooks), as are harpoon arrows and harpoons. The weir used in conjunction with barbasco as a fish poison, baskets, and the gorge for larger fish seem to be the traditional Warao methods.

Although it is mainly considered man's work, women also sometimes engage in fishing, using their bare hands, basketry sieves, gorges, and occasionally fish spears.

The Warao resort only sparingly to piscides. In the first place, the Venezuelan Government has prohibited their use. This, however, is not the chief deterrent. Actually, the Indians are afraid to offend the "Owner of Fish," who, they say, will move away together with all his "people" if too many of them are killed or wasted. The Warao claim, therefore, that they use barbasco poison only in small places, where they hope it may pass unnoticed by the Owner of Fish. A Warao will talk to the Owner of Fish while he waits for his catch, and he will preserve the larger fishbones under the roof of his house to ensure the good will of the Owner of Fish and thereby also his own future luck. Somewhere in the thatch of his roof he also keeps the tooth of a nutria for the same purpose. Pieces of sangrito root are lucky possessions, for it is believed that these were torn off by the Owner of Fish and held in his hand. To protect himself from danger, the fisherman will apply black Saint Andrew's crosses (X) to his harpoon and arrows.

The rivers and lagoons surrounding the settlement of a

particular residential group are considered to be the private
fishing grounds of that group.

From Warao mythology we learn that birds were hunted
from the very beginning, and today the larger birds represent valuable game. Smaller animals, especially rodents
such as agouti and paca, and reptiles, are also considered
acceptable as food. Snakes, however, are not eaten.

The traditional aversion to hunting wild animals—called
"the people of the forest"—is gradually disappearing as a
result of ongoing acculturation, but hunting is still poorly
developed, and many Warao even today will not kill any
of the larger game and will steadfastly refuse to eat of their
flesh. As mentioned, some animals are strictly tabooed;
others are simply avoided. Among the animals hunted by
modern Warao are agouti, paca, baquiro, tapir, deer,
capybara, turtles, and iguana. Feathered game taken include pava, wild turkey, ducks, and parrots. Groups living
close to the estuaries of larger rivers also hunt manatee.
But marsupials, primates, carnivores, and snakes are not
eaten. Of the reptiles only iguana, small alligators, and
turtles are considered good to eat.

In many villages today there is at least one shotgun, but
otherwise the Warao continue to hunt mainly with bow
and arrow. For birds single-point or multipronged arrows
are used; harpoon arrows are employed not only for fish
but also for larger game. Usually, however, the Warao prefer
to hunt large animals with a metal-tipped lance. Rodents
are killed with the harpoon. Hunting is almost exclusively
a male occupation; men hunt in twos or threes but also
combine in larger groups for peccary or agouti drives.
Agouti are driven into hollow logs by groups of hunters
or by especially adept hunting dogs. These dogs are very
important to the Warao, for they spot and flush the animals, even pursuing them across rivers. Sometimes the
women—unarmed—will take off without their men on an

agouti drive of their own, relying exclusively on the hunting dogs.

Except for bird slings, traps are not used as hunting devices, although the "mission" Warao catch paca with sling and shotgun. The Barima River Warao and the Mariusa subtribe build blinds in the tops of trees, set out decoy birds, and thus hidden are able to catch parrots by the dozens, either with a sling or with their bare hands. Their womenfolk or hunting companions wait at the bottom to catch the birds flung down from above, dead from a bite in the neck.

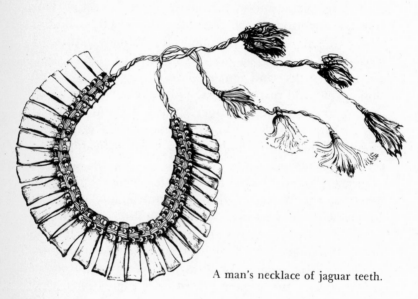

A man's necklace of jaguar teeth.

A hunter will adorn himself with a necklace of jaguar teeth or the teeth of nutria or alligator, previously hidden in some secret place, to ensure his fortune on the hunt. They come into the hunter's possession through the exchange of similar trophies with fellow hunters and are thought to possess considerable magical powers. The hunter who has made the actual kill is regarded as the "owner" of the piece of game, and its meat is distributed according to his instructions.

A menstruating woman exerts negative influence on the hunting and fishing luck of her man. By no means may she touch his weapons or implements, lest they become "useless" and the flesh of the game indigestible. Should any woman in this state touch the gear it is immediately discarded.

It is usually the woman who carries the slain game from boat to kitchen hut. A man who performs this task thereby risks the loss of his hunting powers. We were also told that a hunter will sometimes suffer severe headache during the night, brought on by the slain animal's screaming under the roof of the house. The pain can be alleviated only by the shaman, who blows tobacco smoke over the face and head of the suffering hunter.

The Warao today can best be described as a fishing society with incipient horticulture. The adoption of slash-and-burn horticulture has progressed steadily, albeit sporadically; nowadays there are local groups minimally dependent on the products of their fields, others with intermediate dependence, and still others that rely heavily on the success of their planted crops. Besides such regional differences, there seems also to be an area dependence with respect to the kinds of crops planted. Although, according to contemporary Warao mythology, horticulture had a supernatural origin, the fact is that the majority of the delta Warao lacked any agriculture prior to 1925, when they first came under mission influence. True, in some peripheral regions of the delta, certain local Warao groups were introduced to horticulture by Creoles even prior to the establishment of the first delta mission in 1925, but this early localized exposure seems to have had no major influence on the large body of Warao inhabiting the interior of the delta. The Guyana Warao seem to have lacked agriculture at least until the 1860's; thereafter, judging from early travelers' reports, they appear to have planted food crops only "exceptionally," despite their close association with agricultural Arawak and Carib.

Like the Yanoama, most Warao subgroups terminated their strictly pre-agricultural existence some time during the past hundred years. Many began farming to a significant extent only during the last forty years, and some are still hardly more than accidental horticulturists. Today the Warao grow ocumo, both "bitter" and "sweet" yuca (manioc), corn, bananas, sugar cane, potatoes, and rice. Rice is grown as a cash crop, as is corn on occasion. Ocumo has become a staple Warao food, replacing yuruma almost completely in the strictly nutritional, as opposed to ritual, sense. Bitter manioc and potatoes are of little importance and are not grown in most lower regions of the delta; the same is true of maize. Bananas and plantains, of which some ten varieties are known throughout the delta, represent a relatively important crop. Sugar cane is a great favorite and nowadays is cultivated universally.

The various chores connected with horticulture are divided between husband and wife. The men clear the prospective field shortly before the rainy season and burn the dried trees and brush a month or so later. An individual nuclear family usually owns two or three plots, but men of a residential group will often pool their strength and jointly prepare the fields. Ten to fifteen men will generally labor three or four days to clear an area of approximately 10,000 square meters. Several days after the burning of the fields husband and wife set out seedlings and seeds, using a digging stick to make a hole in the soil and covering it over again with their feet. Harvesting is chiefly women's work, but the men help in hauling the heavy baskets to the boats.

It is taboo for menstruating women to tend their garden plots, nor may they handle the fruits of the field. There are no special rituals pertaining to horticulture as such, but the Warao speak of the "Spirit of the Forest," who appears as they set out to burn the slash of a new clearing and who is appeased by the shaman. The shamans also "blow away" bad weather and storms, lest they damage the village and the crops.

Because of the climate, most foodstuffs cannot be preserved for any length of time. Surplus fish are sometimes roasted or dried in the sun. Morocoto is salted down whenever possible for sale to Creoles and missionaries. Manioc and ocumo will keep for some days; however, little of the former is actually produced, and of the latter there is so much that leftovers are thrown away, for it can easily be prepared at almost any time. Yuruma and a compote of moriche fruit will keep for several weeks without spoiling.

As for food preparation, a good deal is actually eaten raw, including fruit, palm cabbage, sugar cane, larvae, crabs, snails, and reptile eggs. Raw palm cabbage, once the most important provision for long expeditions, is still in great favor. Fish and animals are dressed and roasted, but "true Warao" are reputed to have eaten at least the morocoto without scaling it. Little fish are strung together on a liana and roasted over the embers. Smaller animals, such as acure, paca, and birds, are dressed and cooked on live coals. Ocumo is either sliced and roasted or cut into chunks and boiled in water or fish soup. Yuruma is toasted in little cakes. The use of pots for cooking is a relatively recent practice among the Warao, who originally lacked pottery. Iron pots are now universal throughout the delta. Food is prepared by the women, who spend much of their time around the clay hearth on the kitchen floor. Sometimes they add a little onoto to fish soup. Salt is highly valued but not always available. Honey is used as a sweetener.

The Warao eat "to remain strong." Nursing women eat great amounts of morocoto fish to ensure milk in abundance. The main meals are taken early in the morning and in the late afternoon, although smaller morsels are also eaten at noon and from time to time throughout the day. Meals are always taken in the kitchen houses. The man eats first, then the women and children. Should man and wife eat together, they turn aside from each other or sit back to back. After eating, the adults go to the river, rinse their mouths, and rub the index finger over the teeth.

Food taboos are observed by recently delivered mothers, by sick people and their relatives, and by religious practitioners. Some taboos are temporary, others permanent. Children often receive choice portions, but the elderly are neglected "because they don't need to be strong any more." The shaman must observe several taboos governing the substance as well as the preparation of his food: he may only eat fish and yuruma (ocumo); his first wife must prepare each meal on a new fire; and so on.

Water is the most common drink among the Warao, but although there is water everywhere, it is not always potable. At high tide, brackish water penetrates far into the morichales, and he who is caught there seeks to quench his thirst with the milk contained in the golfball-sized timiche fruit, which is very much like a miniature coconut. The Indians also fell old moriche palms, cut rectangular holes in the trunk, and drain off a sweet juice, which sometimes is left to ferment slightly. A refreshing drink is also made by mascerating the overly ripe fruit of the moriche (and sometimes only the skin of this fruit) with water. A similar drink, known as "wild chocolate" in Guyana, is prepared by boiling the purple fruits of the seje palm, pounding them, and mixing the mash of paper-thin fruit skins with water. Honey water is a most desired drink, as is the fresh juice of sugar cane, which is usually left to ferment. Where bitter yuca is grown the Warao will brew cassiri beer. The Warao of the Barima region brew their cassiri from maize, potatoes, and pineapples. Homemade alcohol is relatively recent among the delta Warao.

Originally tobacco was absent from the delta. Even today it is not grown generally and must be acquired through barter or purchase. In ancient times, smoking was the prerogative of the religious practitioners, who apparently obtained their supply from Trinidad. The deified kanobos (Supreme Spirits that live at the four cardinal points at the ends of the world) are nourished exclusively on smoke, and spirits in general are very fond of it. The ordinary mortal hesitates to smoke in the forest or on the river for fear of attracting a spirit and precipitating an undesirable encounter. By smoking, priest-shamans "travel" to the "houses" of the kanobos. Curing is also effected with the help of tobacco smoke, and large quantities of cigars are consumed during curing sessions. The cigars, 20 to 40 centimeters in length, are made by wrapping tobacco leaves tightly into a stipule of manaca palm. Nowadays cigarettes and tobacco in any form are smoked freely by most Warao; even the women indulge more or less openly as evening falls.

Before the introduction of matches, fire was produced by means of the fire-drill. Nowadays the Warao resort to this traditional method only when absolutely necessary. The fire-drill may be made only by a man and may be used only by a man, who keeps it in his basket or tucked away in the thatch of the roof. Under normal circumstances fire is never allowed to die, not even when the Warao travel long distances. During the day it is kept on the hearth in the kitchen house. The hearth is a great lump of clay, approximately 1 meter in diameter and 30 centimeters thick, packed by the women onto the manaca beams of the kitchen floor. When the members of her family retire to the dwelling house in the evening, the woman carries a burning log from the kitchen to a fireplace under their hammocks. When they make temporary camp in the bush, the Indians do not erect a kitchen house but only a shelter, and the cooking is done right on the forest floor a few meters away. There is no clay hearth, but the logs that support the cooking pot are arranged like the spokes of a wheel.

The Warao also maintain sacred and ritual fires. Such fires (and hearths) are tended in the house of the priest-shaman, at specific locations during the cult festival, and in the menstruation huts. Burning brands of wood and more elaborate torches of beeswax are used for illumination. In those Warao villages where the people have had considerable contact with the Creoles, the women have learned to make short, thick candles. They also use oil lamps, comprising a receptacle of some sort filled with vegetable oil, petroleum, or a mixture of the two, with a floating wick. Pressure lamps and flashlights are rarities, and the only electric lights they have seen are those at the missions or Creole settlements.

The Warao make no economic use of any domestic animal except the dog. Although dogs are now common throughout the entire distribution area of the Warao, the Indians do not seem to have had them in pre-Columbian times. Columbus mentions prehistoric dogs from the West Indies, but the Warao, despite their early relations with Trinidad, appear to have adopted them at a much later date. Actually there is no true Warao term for "dog"; their word, "behoro," seems to be derived from the Spanish "perro." Dogs are kept as watchdogs and hunting dogs.

A woman may also have a favorite dog, which she will breast feed if necessary, and which she will take to the shaman to be cured should it become ill. Should a hunting dog be killed on the hunt, it is mourned, wrapped in a timiche leaf, and buried; but should it die of illness, its carcass is summarily discarded. Warao dogs are consistently ill fed and deliberately mistreated, for a hungry hunting dog is preferred to one that is sated.

The Warao do keep the young of birds and animals around the house, but as pets rather than for economic reasons. However, in recent years they have grown pigs for their Creole neighbors, who pay them for this service. House pets are common, including tame parrots, who scream in unison with their free-flying brothers swooping low over the village; moriche birds in basketry cages; monkeys; sloths; small agouti and paca; and wild ducks and chickens. All these are kept for sheer enjoyment; never is one eaten. Of course, these house animals must fend largely for themselves and rarely live very long. Occasionally they are much-sought-after items in trade.

SOCIAL ORGANIZATION

The Warao do not think of themselves as belonging to one big nation. What combines them in a loose sense as "Warao" is the fact that they all speak the same language and share the same culture. Those who do not are of a different kind, origin, and destiny; they are "Hotarao," people from the higher country.

The most distinct socioeconomic unit of Warao society is the nuclear family, with a father, a mother, and their unmarried children. Generally speaking, marriage is monogamous, but elders and higher ranking men are free to marry two or three women. Co-wives are often consanguineal sisters, and a man may marry the spouse(s) of his defunct brother. Nuclear families tend to cluster together according to a matrilocal rule of residence; this is true especially in the first years of matrimony, during which the young groom has to render bride-service. This is the reason parents wish for girls—because they will bring strong young men into the household through their marriage. Some matrilocal extended families of this kind can muster a considerable labor force, and thus are completely self-sufficient as a local group.

Beyond the extended family, bonds of social organization are very weak. Several extended families may join together as a band, and since the introduction of farming, bands have tended to become larger and to grow into more or less sedentary river communities of several local groups. In pre-agricultural times, bands were loosely held together by a priest-shaman who served a Supreme Being manifested in the form of a sacred stone or some other kind of image. In keeping with colonial tradition, the missionaries introduced the political office of regional gobernador, who has capitanes answering to him, each in charge of a large village, while fiscales are responsible for the small villages. In some communities there is also an arucario, who, like the fiscal, functions as policeman.

The Warao are gradually adapting to this alien system, but there can be no doubt that the paterfamilias of the extended family is still the main authority in the band. Together with his nebu, or sons-in-law, he in turn obeys the orders of the priest-shaman, who speaks with binding religious authority. The concept of purely political power vested in a chief or paramount leader has traditionally been and continues to be an unrealistic one for Warao society. Bands break up quite easily into smaller residential groups. Such splits are triggered by any number of causes, not least the fear that their shamans will attack someone

of their own group. A death occurs in the village; sus-
picions find expression in accusations of sorcery; and the
band disperses.

At one time, pent-up hostilities between neighboring settlements were
released through formal and in part
ritual group duels fought with special combat shields, like the one
shown at right. Opponents clashed
their shields together in an attempt
to throw each other down.

The kinship system of the Warao is of the Hawaiian
type; that is, all cousins are considered to be brothers and
sisters. This reflects the prevailing marriage custom, inasmuch as cousins do not generally marry each other. Marriage partners are chosen from one's own group so that
local endogamy prevails as long as marriageable partners
are available. Descent is reckoned bilaterally, and succession to political or religious office is not subject to any
rigid rules.

LIFE CYCLE AND RELIGIOUS BELIEFS

All Warao men and women consider marriage to be a most natural concomitant of a person's life. Although a young girl may be promised into wedlock at an early age, the marriage may not be consummated before her first menstruation. The Warao are aware that the reproductive cycle of the woman commences with the onset of menstruation and that it is the semen of the man that fertilizes the woman. In mythological times, however, women could conceive without the contribution of a man, and Warao narratives even describe occasions on which men have given birth. Some Warao tell of an earlier world, peopled by only women in one area and only men in another.

Sexual experimentation among Warao children commences fairly early. A boy eight or ten years old will run about attempting to touch the aroused penis of another while the adults watch unconcernedly. Masturbation is permitted among children of both sexes. Premarital sex is practiced, especially in those regions where the marriage ceremony is minimal—amounting to scarcely more than overtly moving one person's hammock next to that of another. A man publicly expresses affection by draping his arm over the girl's shoulder and stroking her arm. Kissing is unknown, although a mother will sometimes press her lips tenderly to her baby's forehead.

The men consider light-skinned women especially attractive. Other attributes of beauty in a female are high eyebrows, abundant hair, small cheek bones, small, firm breasts, a narrow waist, wide hips, strong thighs, small feet, and a sparse growth of pubic hair. To enhance her beauty, a woman will oil her hair, paint her forehead with onoto, pluck her eyebrows, and draw them in again with paint. Women try to acquire as many silver and glass-bead ornaments as possible. The ideal man has a tall, lean, mus-

cular, and agile body. In public, men and women are
ashamed to expose the genital area, but exposure of the
bare female breast is considered quite natural. Unless
married to each other, members of the two sexes do not
bathe together.

A man who is attracted to a woman will make his intentions known by staring fixedly at her. Should such
overt courting fail, he may secretly ask a shaman to sing
a particular chant that is supposed to have an aphrodisiac
effect. Sexual license is sometimes observed during the
various festivals, but this is frowned upon. Children born
to unwed girls as a consequence of such encounters are not
discriminated against, and a more permanent relationship
usually develops between the two parents as a result of the
birth.

Reference to various homosexual acts can be found in
the oral literature of the Warao. Women masturbate with
an artificial phallus; men carve "women" out of banana
trees. Male transvestites have occasionally been observed—
a phenomenon said to run in certain families. A transvestite supposedly believes that he would perish if he dressed
and acted as a man. Sometimes a transvestite appears to live
in union with a man. No case of female transvestism has
yet come to our attention. Transvestites are not persecuted
in Warao society.

The Warao relate menstruation to the Moon, who, as
a young man, had an incestuous relationship with his
sister and was punished by transformation. Menstruation
is believed to have a debilitating effect on the male sex,
various activities, and certain inanimate objects. A husband suffers weakness during the time when his wife has
her menses and finds that he cannot lift a heavy load.
Should a man have intercourse with a woman in this
condition he would fall sick or become enfeebled for the
rest of his life; so strong is the taboo that a shaman would

perish if he had intercourse with a menstruating woman and would lose his hearing should a menstruating woman address him. A woman is considered "unclean" during the days of her period and hence isolates herself in a special hut. The fire she uses is tabooed; she may not touch any tools or weapons, or go to the fields. A woman who commences menstruating while on a river journey must take special precautions. She rubs her body with fragrant herbs and retreats to the bow of the boat behind a screen of timiche leaves, lest the water spirits stop the dugout and pull it beneath the surface. When her period is over, the woman leaves the menstruation hut, cleanses herself with a ritual bath, and rejoins society.

The Warao believe that the black fruit of a particular tree favors fertilization, and that the same fruit causes conception when eaten in large quantities. A compote of moriche fruit is also eaten by young women to hasten conception and is studiously avoided if a child is not desired. Effective contraceptives do not seem to be available to Warao women. Female sterility is rare; these unfortunate few who are sterile are called "snake women."

Infanticide is usually practiced only in the case of malformed newborns, which the Warao believe to be the offspring of spirits. To avoid subsequent conception after the death of a child, a woman will close the ears and nose of the little corpse and bury it face down, as well as abstain from moriche fruit. Twins are said to be acceptable. Although Warao always hope that the firstborn will be a male, in general daughters are preferred, for they can help their mothers about the house, and their marriage, as noted, will bring another male into the household to assist the father.

Pregnant women abstain from yuruma and moriche juice. Food taboos are relaxed somewhat during the last month before term, however, when the woman may also avoid the more strenuous chores.

Birth takes place in the menstruation hut if the family is in its permanent settlement, or behind a windscreen if they are away from home. The woman in labor is assisted by her mother and other female relatives. One woman holds the parturient under the shoulders and two others clasp her knees. In each community there are women who are known for their experience as midwives; these are consulted before delivery and asked to assist on the occasion itself. The husband is allowed to assist at the birth only in the absence of any female help. Otherwise he waits silently in the house. The other men, women, and children usually leave the village altogether. The village shaman may stay behind to help the laboring woman, if necessary, by singing and blowing tobacco smoke. If labor continues for any length of time, the mother is given a potion of warm water mixed with sangrito ashes, a drink producing vomiting and violent convulsions.

For the actual birth, the mother squats, and the baby is delivered onto a padding of timiche leaves placed beneath her. The umbilical cord is cut with a knife of timiche wood. In Guyana the mother is reputed to sever the cord by biting through it. The newborn is washed and placed in a baby sling, and the mother is bathed with warm water. Stillborn babies are buried in the cemetery. The Mongolian spot is commonly seen on the newborn, and moles are called "blood of the moon."

The new father observes so-called couvade restrictions for about two weeks; i.e., he may move about the village, but it is considered more advantageous for the child's health if the father keeps to his hammock as much as possible and avoids strenuous activity. Under no circumstances may he eat game during this period.

An infant will teethe easily if the mother has buried the

placenta properly. Soon after delivery she digs a hole about 50 centimeters deep in which she places the placenta, the blood, and the timiche leaf padding. She closes the hole with the heel of her foot and covers the entire surface with ashes. If a woman wishes to end her fertility, she secretly ties five knots in the umbilical cord still attached to the placenta before she buries it. To reinforce the effort she kisses both little fingers and both little toes of the infant.

A husband may construct a more elaborate "birth house" within the village compound shortly before his wife delivers. Actual delivery, however, never takes place here. The woman and her newborn child move from the menstruation hut into the birth house and remain there for a few days before rejoining the rest of the family in its dwelling. In the birth house, mother and child are visited by the women of the village only, never by the men. On returning to the village some mothers paint their cheeks and foreheads red and oil their hair. To resume intercourse sooner than one full month after delivery is considered dangerous—for the father.

Abortions are performed if the father of the child should die during his wife's pregnancy, if a young girl seeks to terminate her pregnancy, or if a woman simply does not want another child. Drinking the juice of acid fruits mixed with the fruit of the timiche palm is said to induce abortion, but a more effective method is to squeeze and pound the abdomen itself. The fetus is thrown into the forest to ensure its rebirth—for in the river it would drown and be forever lost.

The baby is nursed practically from the moment of its birth, whenever it wants the breast, and continues nursing at least until the appearance of its first teeth. In some cases children continue to take the breast until they are four or even five years old. Women with small breasts massage them with salt water during the last months of pregnancy and will also drink a salt solution two or three times after delivery. The nursing mother abstains from oil and certain fish, which are believed to cause diarrhea in the baby. Surplus milk is pressed out from the breast by massage and pulling the nipple.

The baby's first tooth makes its appearance at the age of seven to eight months and is immediately pulled out and put into a plant by the father, for the Warao believe that otherwise no further teeth will grow. At approximately one and a half years of age, the child is given the first solid food of bananas, ocumo, or fish, prechewed by the mother. Children start to walk between the ages of one and two years and are either helped by the mother, who supports the baby under the arms, or left to learn by themselves. A small child is cared for intensively by his mother and sleeps in her hammock until he is four or five years of age, unless a younger sibling "pushes him out" into his own hammock. Small children and babies are bathed every day and are carried about by their mothers in baby slings. Generally, the children are treated affectionately by their parents. A father plays with his offspring, especially the small ones. Children are rarely punished, but should one throw a tantrum, he is doused with water or simply pushed into the river, whence he calmly returns to warm himself at the fire.

After six years of age, the children participate fully in the daily routine of the village. Boys go with their fathers and the girls remain with their mothers to learn the Warao lifeway. Parents are criticized publicly if their children misbehave, if they fail (after the age of two) to use the proper latrine, or if they play too much. Older children are expected to be self-reliant and responsible for their younger siblings as well. Should a child find himself in an alarming predicament—for instance, if his dugout has tipped over—he expects no assistance from his parents but may be certain of ridicule from the other adults. Among siblings, and also among individuals of the same generation, strong alliances are formed which provide some measure of cohesion throughout the rest of their lives.

There are no special ceremonies marking a boy's entrance into manhood. The Warao consider a boy a man when he can perform a man's tasks. Parents boast of the perseverance, courage, and strength of their adolescent son, claiming that he is already an adult—and growing pubic hair!

A puberty ceremony for a girl takes place on the occasion of her first menstruation at the age of twelve or thirteen. She is secluded in the menstruation hut (nowadays it is more often a special corner reserved for this purpose in the dwelling house), where she must not leave her hammock on her own or touch her feet to the ground under any circumstances. Twice daily a man and woman— a couple unrelated to her but referred to as step-parents— appear to carry the child to a special seat outside the house. The women of the village pour water over her as she sits; this is believed to ensure fertility. She must observe silence for three days, and her sole diet consists of the traditional "true" food: yuruma and morocoto fish. She may drink water. Her hair is cropped, gathered in a basket, and buried. This is supposed not only to guarantee uncomplicated deliveries in the future, but also to forestall the premature sickening and death of the girl's parents. Her back is painted in geometrical designs, circles, and Saint Andrew's crosses. She is given a glass-bead necklace by her parents, to be worn from that day on, and is considered a marriageable young woman. She may marry a much older man, usually as his second wife, or she may be given to a young man sixteen to eighteen years of age.

Group exogamy is permitted, but endogamy appears to prevail.

Marriage usually requires the consent of the young woman, as well as of her parents. The young man goes to the headman, who shouts the important question to the girl's parents across the entire length of the village. Thus the public is informed; members of the girl's extended family may add their advice as well. If they object to the match it is usually because they do not consider the boy to be capable of properly caring for a wife and family, and they loudly voice their opposition by shouting that they have "enough children to feed." The prospective groom is asked to assure the community formally that he knows how to care for his future family. Then the girl's mother slings the groom's hammock next to that of her daughter. There is no further formal ceremony.

Bride-price is unknown, but bride-service is performed, especially during the first years of marriage. Secondary marriages (after mutual consent is obtained) are sealed by having the woman move into the house of the man, where she will sling her hammock next to his, on the other side from his first wife. Polygamy is often of the sororal type. The levirate (marriage of a woman to her defunct husband's brother) is also practiced, although under certain circumstances a widow may choose a husband other than her dead husband's brother. Divorce is relatively simple: the partners separate. Small children remain with the mother, while the older ones have the choice of going with either parent.

A person is considered "old" when his dependence on the younger generation reaches a certain point. He lives with one or another of his children and is never treated very well by any of them. An old woman will try to remain useful by busying herself with the manufacture of yet another hammock. The old are ridiculed for any of a number of habits peculiar to them, and they are often beaten when their nagging, complaining, and begging become unbearable.

According to Warao belief, all illness can be traced to supernatural or magical causes; even accidents are ascribed in an indirect way to such externalized agents. Sickness is believed to be caused by one or another of the deified kanobos, who thereby expresses his dissatisfaction with man. This kind of sickness is referred to as hebu. Children especially suffer from such attacks. The type of priest-shaman known as wisiratu is the only one who can intervene as curer. Other sicknesses, called hoa, are caused by magic of "black" shamans, called hoarotu, who spread illness and death among their enemies. Only a friendly hoarotu can effect a cure in this case. Finally, still other illnesses are caused by the introduction of magical arrows (hatabu) into the victim by a hostile bahanarotu: a friendly bahanarotu can assuage such misfortune through massage and blowing.

A Warao rarely treats himself. A father may have to open an abscess on his child with a wooden dagger of manaca. A mother will force open the eyelid of a small child, apply her mouth to the eye itself, and spit in it to wash out a painful foreign body. The pangs of toothache are relieved by applying heat; if that fails, the tooth is extracted with the fingers. The warm urine of children (three to eight years old and of opposite sex to the patient) is recommended for catarrh, as are various potions of moriche water, fruits and shoots, lemon herbs and water, or pieces of liana mixed with the leaves of a very small moriche palm. Shoots of the timiche palm are crushed, mixed with water, and rubbed over the head and chest of the victim. Catarrh is a major killer among the Warao, and most of the remedies reflect their helplessness and despair. The same is true for intestinal disorders. Anyone can prepare the various medicines, such as they are, but the illness of hebu, hoa, and hatabu can be cured only by the appropriate practitioner, who derives his power from metaphysical and psychic sources.

The Warao hold that blood is the carrier of life. A baby comes to be through the blood of the mother and the semen of the father. Life ends if too much blood is lost, or if it coagulates and grows cold, the cooling of the blood being manifested in the cessation of respiration.

Suicide is rare and is thought to occur usually as the result of excessive grief or extreme jealousy. Some commit suicide by strangulation, and Warao folk literature describes death as a result of the person's dunking his head in a pot of hot water.

When death occurs naturally, the entire household gathers about the dying relative, encouraging him to "stay" and asking him who was to blame for the tragedy. In the course of the interrogation, hebu, hoa, and hatabu are cited as possible causative agents, and a practitioner suspected of sending the illness may be identified and later brought to trial. Hebu deaths occur as long as it pleases the kanobos to send hebu. The annual moriche festival propitiates the kanobos and is believed to ward off the deaths of many children. Hoa may kill several people in the same village before the enemy hoarotu practitioner turns away to pursue his evil intentions elsewhere. The arrows (hatabu) of the bahanarotu also may claim victims for a long period of time.

After his final breath, the hammock of the dead person is lowered to touch the floor of the house, and the shell trumpet is blown to summon all his friends to the funeral. The mourners sit for a while beside the hammock, separated according to sex. Sometimes a relative will paint the corpse's face and hair red with onoto, or tie a piece of white cloth around the head of the defunct and paint a red cross on it. The belongings of the dead are placed in his hammock with him, the hammock is strung on a pole, and two men carry it to the boat, while the women continue loud wailing and screaming. The guests follow in their boats to the cemetery. Here the corpse is placed in a hollowed-out tree, a coffin which rests either on two wooden forks or on a platform of manaca beams. The hammock is slipped from under the body and is buried separately. The coffin is covered with timiche leaves and layers of mud tightly secured with lianas. A more or less elaborate roof is constructed over the coffin of a dignitary. Normally, friends and relatives, with the possible exception of parents, will not return to the grave. However, if the death was laid to the malevolent interference of a hoarotu, the priest-shaman of the village will go again the next day to inspect the grave for telltale marks that will give the "murderer" away. They look especially for footprints because it is believed that the spirit of such a shaman will walk to the grave site at night to mock the dead person.

At the death of a small child, the close relatives come to mourn while the little corpse rests on the lap of a kinswoman. Several hours later, an uncle or an aunt will carry it to the cemetery and deposit the body in a wooden box or a small, hollowed-out tree trunk. The small hammock is buried separately near a tree or else is taken home to be kept by the parents in a safe place. Several children may be buried in the same box if multiple deaths occur in quick succession.

The Warao practice secondary burial. After the flesh of the corpse has decomposed, the bones are removed and placed in a short piece of hollowed-out tree trunk. The Mariusa Warao exhume the dead after three months, and then keep the bones in baskets hung from the beams of a special house constructed close to their village. This prac-

A casket used for secondary burial.

tice may have had a more extensive distribution in times past.

Life does not terminate with death. A man's soul lives on, and, to ensure its sustenance, food and drink are deposited next to the grave. The souls of the dead roam about the dwelling places they have known in life. There are some Warao who believe that the soul, or some part of it, will be reborn in human form. But the soul of the shaman goes to live with his mentor Supreme Being, and the soul of a master canoe builder travels across the sky to live forever with his "protector" spirit.

Much of a Warao Indian's life is spent in propitiating the numerous Supreme Spirits that live at the four cardinal points at the ends of the world. These kanobos request nourishment in form of tobacco smoke from the people. The priest-shaman (wisiratu) may visit them in his dreams or in a trance, under the influence of tobacco, and on returning from such a visit transmits the message of that particular Supreme Spirit to his community. One of the three major spirits at the cardinal points is usually present among the people in form of a stone, which the priest-shaman, the Guardian of the Sacred Stone, keeps in a special box-like basket within the shrine or temple. An-nually the kanobos are invited from the ends of the world to reside within the temple. Here they submerge in a barrel of yuruma prepared as a sacrificial offering by the community. The kanobos are said to enjoy passing time smoking in the temple, and later to participate (through

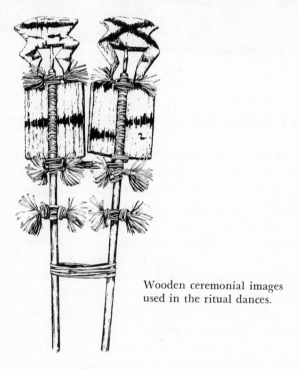

Wooden ceremonial images used in the ritual dances.

wooden images planted in the middle of the dancing platform) in the ritual dances. The annual yuruma or moriche festival (nahanamu), presided over by the priest-shaman, is celebrated in propitiation—upon request by the Supreme Spirit, who will protect the community if his command is heeded.

The "white" shaman (bahanarotu) presides over an ancient cult of fertility, called habisanuka. He travels in his dream or trance and under the influence of tobacco to an eastern part of the celestial dome. The celestial bridge which he frequents and maintains between his community and these eastern Spirits guarantees abundance of life on earth. The "black" shaman (hoarotu) maintains the otherwise severed connection between the Warao and dark powers of the West who live through their medium, the black shaman, from the blood and the flesh of man.

Both forms of shamanism represent very old forms of religion, of possible Eurasian origin. The priest-shaman temple-idol cult of the moriche festival is reminiscent of circum-Caribbean cults as practiced in these regions by Indians of various chiefdoms. It also contains many features of the religious life and cults of the more advanced civilizations of Central and Southwestern America. Like the Chibchan characteristics of the Warao language, the cult directs our attention to this general part of the New World as the possible point of more recent origin of these Indians. A true Warao community cannot exist without this very powerful shamanistic religion. Its loss would seriously disturb the social and psychic equilibrium of the community and eventually that of the entire society. It represents a very special elaboration of Warao culture, and its undermining through Creole and mission contact will probably dislocate this *axis mundi* of the Warao seriously enough to put an end to one of the most ancient and successful surviving autochthonous cultures in South America.

BIBLIOGRAPHY

Barral, Basilio Maria de, *Los Indios Guaraúnos y su Cancionera*. Biblioteca "Missionalia Hispánica," XV. Madrid: 1964.

Moreno, A. Turrado, *Etnografía de los Indios Guaraúnos.* Caracas: Lithografía y Tipografía Vargas, 1945.

Sociedad de Ciencias Naturales La Salle, Caracas, "Informe Preliminar de la Segunda Expedición al Delta del Orinoco" (29.7-27.8, pp. 9-12). Manuscript. Caracas: 1945.

Suarez, Maria Matilde, "La Organización Social de los Warao," *Acta Científica Venezolana,* XXI, 4 (1970), 135-38.

Wilbert, Johannes, "Los Instrumentos Musicales de los Indios Warrau (Guarao, Guaraúno)," *Antropológica,* No. 1 (1956), 2-22.

———, "Die soziale und politische Organisation der Warrau," *Kölner Zeitschrift für Soziologie und Sozialpsychologie,* X, 2 (1958), 272-91.

———, "Vestidos y Adornos de los Indios Warao," *Antropológica,* No. 12 (1964), 6-26.

———, *Folk Literature of the Warao Indians.* Latin American Studies, XV. Los Angeles: University of California, Los Angeles, 1970.

———, "Tobacco and Shamanistic Ecstasy Among the Warao Indians," in Peter T. Furst, ed., *Flesh of the Gods: The Ritual Use of Hallucinogens.* New York: Praeger, 1972.

ETHNOGRAPHIC FILMS

Copies of films 1 and 2 may be ordered from Institut für den Wissenschaftlichen Film, 34 Göttingen, Nonnstieg 72, Germany.

1. *Kampfspiel mit Schilden (Seraio).* ("Fighting Game with Shields [Sereio].") Luis T. Laffer. 1957. 3 min. Color.
2. *Rituelle Tänze.* ("Ritual Dances.") Luis T. Laffer, 1957. 4½ min. Color.

Copies of films 3 and 4 may be ordered from the Latin American Center, University of California, Los Angeles, California 90024.

3. *The Warao.* Jorge Preloran. 1970. 58 min. Color, sound, 16 mm.

A feature-length documentary about the Warao Indians

of the Orinoco Delta in Venezuela. The film shows the
daily life of these Indians, only recently in contact with the
modern world.

4. *Mosori Monika.* C. Strand. 1969. 20 min. Color, sound,
16 mm. (Rental: $30, purchase: $300.)

Shows the missionaries' deep influence on Indian life
style and the dilemmas of acculturation. Narrated by a
nun and an old Warao woman, the film explores the think-
ing of both and the ways in which changes in material
culture have changed Indian attitudes.

4 The Cultivators: The Makiritare of Territorio Amazonas

With the development of horticulture, a whole new epoch of cultural development began in Venezuela. The domestication of yuca, one of the most important discoveries made by prehistoric man in lowland South America, may have originated in the general area of Venezuela late in the Meso-Indian period some three thousand years ago. Corn planting and the cultivation of associated crops diffused from western South America to the tribes of western Venezuela. Horticulture based on yuca and root crops gave rise to a tropical-forest kind of gardening, which facilitated the growth and expansion of such Neo-Indian tribes as the Carib and Arawak across Venezuela and northern South America. The development of full-scale horticulture represented an enormous advance in Indian cultural evolution, the impetus for which grew during the Meso-Indian period, when changing ecological and cultural conditions confronted early man in Venezuela with the question of his very survival. During the horticultural Neo-Indian period (3,000 to 1,500 B.P.), however, Venezuela lagged behind other parts of the New World in cultural development. A number of cultures in the western part of the country were basically similar to the typical Neo-Indian formative cultures of Colombia, Peru, and Mexico. But the characteristic features of these advanced cultures and indigenous civilizations were only weakly developed, if at all.

Some Venezuelan Neo-Indian societies survive to the present: the Makiritare of the Territorio Amazonas, the Yupa of the Sierra de Perijá, the Panare of the Cuchivero region, and the Pemon of the Gran Sabana.

THE HABITAT

The tribal name "Makiritare" is the common Venezuelan designation for the Yecuana Indians, who inhabit parts of the Territorio Amazonas between 3° and 5° North latitude and 63° and 66° West longitude. "Makiritare," apparently an Arawakan term meaning "river people," has been used so profusely throughout the literature that we adopt it for purposes of this description rather than the Indian's own designations "Yecuana" or "Soto."

One can distinguish three main subgroups of Makiritare according to their geographic distribution: the people of the Erebato, the Upper Ventuari, and the Cunucunuma River. Some groups have also been reported in the adjacent Brazilian territory, including the river valleys of the Parime, Auari, and Upper Uraricuera. Most, however, appear to have migrated northward into Venezuela. Of the various Cariban tribes that once inhabited the Territorio Amazonas, only the Makiritare survive as a major tribal society. The total Makiritare population numbers between 1,200 and 1,600 individuals, located in some thirty village communities.

The distribution area of the Makiritare covers a portion of the Guyana continental shelf, which features elevations in excess of 2,000 meters. The Indians prefer the valleys of the major rivers for their actual settlements and remain mostly in the lowlands some 200 to 500 meters above sea level. But the general hunting grounds of the tribe are situated at elevations of 500 to 1,500 meters. Tropical-forest growth, broken intermittently by a patchwork of savannas, covers most of the area. The trees reach 20 to 50 meters into the sky with trunks up to 2 meters in diameter. The Makiritare tend to avoid the savannas, which are heavily infested with mosquitoes and gnats and which, they say, harbor evil fevers. The savannas of the Upper Kuntinama, as well as the mountain system Marawaka–Druida–Kushamakari, are considered out of bounds for religious reasons.

The three Makiritare subgroups inhabiting this general area remain in close contact with one another by maintaining an efficient network of jungle paths connecting the headwaters of the various major rivers—the Caura, Erebato, Ventuari, Cunucunuma, and others. These rivers, together with their tributaries, serve the Indians as highways. But while the Indians use the waterways with great facility, the numerous rapids and waterfalls have effectively prevented the white man from invading Makiritare territory. The major falls present insurmountable walls behind which the Makiritare have been safe from white penetration. In fact, because of the inaccessibility of their habitat, the Conquest became reality for the Makiritare only during the late eighteenth century.

Relatively amicable initial contact with members of the Solano Border Commission following the year 1756 whetted the appetite of the Makiritare for the goods of the Spaniards. Avid for metal tools, they established a fairly intensive trading relationship with the town of Angostura (Ciudad Bolívar) on the Lower Orinoco. But the Indians visited the white man in his own territory when they wished to do so, and on their own terms. Later, in 1765, when missionaries came to proselytize them, and still later, when an ambitious governor opened a fortified road straight through Makiritare territory, the Indians rebelled. They put the torch to the fortifications and found safety once more in the inaccessible reaches behind the falls. Thus the Spaniards to the north of the Makiritare and the Dutch of Guyana remained only distant trading partners. Contact, directly or indirectly through intermediates, occurred on terms dictated by the Indians themselves, who literally fled from the ruthless exploiters of the short-lived rubber boom in the Ventuari and Cunucunuma regions. Only the material goods of the white man were welcome, and these were present throughout the villages long before most of the Indians (especially the women and children) came to realize that the whites were real people and not the fictive creations of their oral literature.

The pattern of visiting the settlements of the white man and retreating again to a jungle stronghold remained consistent until the 1950's, when Protestant and Catholic missionaries succeeded in establishing themselves among the Makiritare. However, the process of cultural change, through contact with the Europeans, had begun back in 1756. Since there was no sustained contact, these influences affected only the indigenous technology and material culture, leaving the socioeconomic and autochthonous value systems largely unaltered.

Linguistic changes were similarly of a minor nature; even today few persons know any Spanish. Instead, the various subgroups of the Makiritare all speak the same language of Cariban affiliation. Geographical distance among the subgroups has perpetuated marked dialectical differences, but nowhere do these impede mutual intelligibility.

MATERIAL CULTURE AND TECHNOLOGY

The red cloth and small glass beads of the white man, as well as his iron tools, catch the eye of the Makiritare trader. The women, especially those living close to the frontier, use the red fabric to fashion tunic-like dresses, while the men reserve a strip of the same material 25 centimeters wide and about 2 meters long to use as a breech-clout. The strip is passed between the legs, wrapped around the loins, and fastened to a waist string. The front end piece covers the pubic area like a short, rectangular apron. In the back the free end hangs to the knees or even as far as the heels. Should a woman lack sufficient material for an entire dress, she makes do with a small piece 25 centimeters square, fastened around the loins with string and tied in the back. The minuscule cover closely resembles its barkcloth precursor, originally worn by both men and women. Nudity is never considered shameful, and even if an Indian owns clothes he will never hesitate to strip down to the pubic cover in pursuit of his daily activities. Children run completely naked until the age of eight or ten and then put on the loincloth typical for their sex. Sometimes a child is made to wear a waist string even before he is old enough to wear a loincloth, as a reminder of his approaching adolescence.

In the early years of contact, the women learned how to make very decorative aprons of glass beads, and it is quite possible that quartz and stone beads may have served the same purpose even earlier. Beaded aprons were sometimes rectangular but more often trapezoidal, with an upper width of 30 centimeters and a lower width of 45. The upper and lower edges of the apron are decorated with red, blue, and white geometrical designs and zoomorphic patterns symbolizing frogs and monkeys. The section between the decorative bands is left entirely white or blue. The woman fastens this beautiful apron around her waist with a string and ties a number of dried seed pods to each lower corner, which rustle when she walks and dances. The beads of red, white, and blue glass are also fashioned into various other adornments for both men and women.

Generally speaking, women routinely wear more orna-
mentation than do the men, who decorate themselves on
festive occasions only. Necklaces made of bands of glass
beads 6 or 7 centimeters wide are worn by both sexes. Men

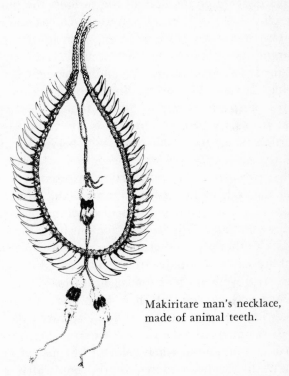

Makiritare man's necklace,
made of animal teeth.

and women also sling long strands of beads diagonally
across the torso. The glass beads on the strand are interspersed with seeds and pods of various plants, cotton tassels, colorful feathers, monkey teeth, anteater claws, and
deer hoofs. Women wear earrings made of relatively large
triangular silver plates hanging from the earlobes on a
double string of beads. Men sometimes wear similar
earrings of a crescent shape, reserving the triangular silver

plates for use on neckwear only. More frequently seen on the men is the handsome ear decoration made from a 15-centimeter-long piece of arrowgrass, in one end of which is inserted a plug of trimmed toucan feathers arranged in concentric rings of black and yellow. The arrowgrass plug is passed through the hole in the earlobe, the plumed end hanging down in front almost to the collarbone.

The Makiritare place great emphasis on decorating the extremities. Women, and even men, favor wristlets of strung white glass beads. But more frequently they wind strings of the white beads, finger-woven cotton bands, or strips of sturdy vegetable fiber around the upper arm. The bands are tied very firmly, as are similar decorations worn around the ankle and just below the knee. So tightly are they drawn that biceps and calf muscles bulge below them and become permanently prominent, a feature that the Indians find most admirable and worth the pain caused by the ligatures. Muscle deformation commences at an early age, with parents admonishing their children to ignore the pain. Sometimes the women make their arm- and legbands of beads. In the not too distant past the men used women's hair for leg ligatures.

Men and women cut their hair short all around the head, leaving most of the forehead and half the ears covered. Normally the Makiritare wear no headdress except on festive occasions, when colorful bunches of piapoco or macaw feathers are placed in the hair. Men also wear crowns of long macaw feathers sewn to a doughnut-shaped base of woven lianas or bamboo bark. The same ring serves as the base of a less elaborate headdress made by fastening small toucan feathers and macaw tail feathers vertically to the back of the crown. For gala purposes the men don skirts made of palm leaves fastened to a liana belt.

Body painting is of great cosmetic importance to both sexes. Onoto is the principal source of red paint. The onoto seeds are boiled down in water, and the residual paste is mixed with seje oil before use. In addition to onoto, the Makiritare also use the leaves of a liana, extracting the red color by boiling and mixing the residue with palm oil or resin. A dark brown color is produced from the latex of a plant called tununu, and dark blue dye is obtained from the fruit of the genipapo.

The women use body paint more often than do the men. Both sexes decorate their faces almost daily with geometrical linear and curvilinear designs, but the women paint their torsos, arms, and legs, as well. No matter how small they are, the children are often painted by their mothers. Men apply the brown paint on festive occasions; again, the women use this more frequently. Blue is the color for proclamation. An ambassador, for instance, will paint a blue bar from ear to ear across his mouth and lips. The

A stamp used for body decoration.

Makiritare use small sticks or roller "stamps" carved from wood to apply the paint. Depilation is practiced by all adults, who remove eyebrows and other body hair more or less thoroughly.

One of the most outstanding accomplishments of the Makiritare is their basketry craftsmanship, almost wholly a male occupation. The sole item made by women—and for their own use only—is the cylindrical basket for carrying yuca. Although the commonly available basic basket material is itiriti or manare, the Makiritare prefer to use bamboo strips, from which they weave outstanding pieces, both monochrome and multicolored. First the bamboo strips, of equal width, are cleaned of their green outer

surface. Some are left a natural yellow, others are dyed
black with soot, and still others are dyed a reddish ochre
with onoto. The colors are fixed by means of resinous
shavings from the bark of the adukuni tree. Woven
products include mats, carrying baskets, knapsacks, tele-
scoping two-piece rectangular containers (to store household goods), round shallow trays, tubular yuca presses
(sebucanes), yuca sifters, fire fans, bags for collecting wild
foods, bucket-shaped utility baskets, conical baskets (for
landing fish), and bird cages. The basic techniques employed are twilled weaving, checkerboard, and wicker-
work.

All Makiritare men know how to weave baskets. A
young man will first try his hand at a yuca press, an indispensable household item. But nowadays the true artisan of
basketry can be found only among the old, and even among
them there are few now who have achieved perfection in
the craft. They know how to edge the various types of
baskets properly, have mastered the proportions for vary-

A carrying basket and a woven fire fan.

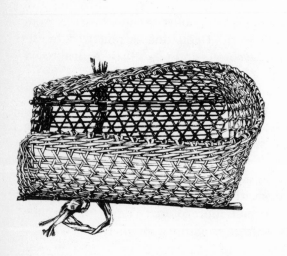

ing diameters, and have learned to depict in two dimensions various significant representations of their own real
world. This is particularly important for the weaving of
zoomorphic designs onto the surface of the rectangular
storage baskets and the round trays. The zoomorphic designs, passed from one generation to the next, derive from
Makiritare mythology. The thematic content and execu-
tion are discussed at length among the artisans, especially
when the subject matter is a design developed in a singular
manner by a particular artist. More than thirty major
varieties of such traditional motifs are known to the
Makiritare weavers, including representations of the water
snake, the frog, the mythical Sacred Monkey who brought
yuca into the world, and the constellations.

Strangely enough, Makiritare women are excluded from
this artistic realm. The wicker baskets produced by women
serve only for everyday transporting purposes (holding upwards of 120 pounds of yuca tubers) and are carried with
a tumpline, as are all carrying baskets and knapsacks. The
women, however, imitate the artistry of the men in the
fabrication of their glass-bead aprons, whose upper and
lower decorative bands frequently show zoomorphic designs. In a manner peculiar to Guayana tribes, the women
use a D-shaped frame of two sticks on which they weave the
apron. The beads are strung on two horizontal weft threads
between which the warps pass vertically. In this way the
fill remains compact and of identical appearance on both
sides.

The women also spin thread from cultivated cotton,
using an exceptionally long spindle, from 70 to more than
100 centimeters in length. The shaft is provided with a
planar, convex, wooden discoid whorl and is rotated almost
horizontally between the palm of the woman's hand and
her right thigh. Makiritare yarns are spun to the left and
often combine the initial single-ply yarn with two, three,

or four others to make a strong multi-ply string. Many women excel at spinning fine, uniform strands, which are wound in a ball and given to the husband for the fabrication of a hammock.

Cotton yarn is used principally to make hammocks and finger-woven bands. Loom weaving is completely unknown among the Makiritare, but the men make the so-called barred hammock by winding a continuous spiral of cotton string between two upright poles sunk in the ground, with a separation corresponding to the desired length of the hammock. A horizontal pole is tied to the top of each upright to stabilize the frame. The warp strings are intertwined every 10 centimeters with a weft bar of four strands. Upon completion, the hammock is slipped off the two posts, and ropes are attached to each end. Baby slings are usually made of bast, less frequently of finger-woven cotton string. The men produce strong ropes by twisting curagua fiber. Finer string of the same basic material is used to fabricate funnel-shaped landing nets mounted on round frames. Palm leaves are often folded to carry fruit, insects, and other small foodstuffs.

Traditionally men have always been the potters among the Makiritare, but nowadays old women have been observed making pots. With the introduction of metal containers, the art of pottery is degenerating, as clay articles fall increasingly into disuse. Unlike Yanoama pottery, the plain, utilitarian, casserole-shaped vessel of the Makiritare is not made by the coiling technique but by a method resembling direct molding. The nearly flat bottom is shaped from a lump of clay, and the walls are built up by adding successive pinches. After the modeling is complete, both inside and outside are smoothed with a splinter of wood or a piece of calabash. The pot is dried in the sun or close to the hearth and fired in the open. The blackened ware is sometimes polished with a piece of jasper or else glazed slightly by throwing resin into the flames.

Calabashes play an important role in every Makiritare household, serving as bottles, dishes, ladles, and spoons. The inside is painted onoto-red or black with a mixture of soot and rubber latex, vegetable oil, or resin. The resulting surface takes a high polish. The outside of the calabash is natural yellow, decorated in various geometrical or zoomorphic designs with a brownish dye from the resin of the ayawa tree. An artistically inclined man will often incise the soft surface of the green calabash in a geometrical design or dotted pattern.

Originally the Makiritare used bows and arrows for hunting and warfare. Possession of firearms first came in the middle of the eighteenth century on initial contact with the whites. Increased distribution and familiarity with such weapons through the years—from the ancient harquebus of the Spaniards and Dutch to the modern shotgun—together with the adoption of the blowgun, have brought about a gradual loss of proficiency as archers. The Makiritare is ridiculed for his ineptness by his Yanoama neighbors, but he looks to the Yanoama to supply him with a better bow than he himself could make.

The typical Makiritare bow is 1.40 to 1.80 meters in length, and 2 centimeters in cross-section at the middle, tapering to pointed ends. Made of a species of caoba, the bow is heavy, reddish brown, and very smooth once it has been thoroughly rubbed down with sand and polished with abrasive emery leaves. The bow is reinforced with a surplus length of bowstring carried in a groove along the back. Shooting short distances only (mostly for fishing purposes), the Makiritare deploy mainly iron-tipped harpoon arrows. The forepiece of the harpoon arrow is longer and the arrowgrass shaft thicker than the corresponding parts of a different single-piece arrow also used by the Makiritare.

Calabash water bottles, dishes, ladles and spoons.

The smaller arrow carries a barbed iron head obtained from the neighboring Pemon of the Gran Sabana. The end of the nock of a composite arrow is inserted into the reed shaft and fastened firmly with fine cotton thread and resin adhesive. The arrows are almost as long as the bow, measuring some 1.50 meters, and are usually feathered tangentially. Large game is killed with a 1.60-meter-long metal-tipped lance.

The principal hunting weapon of the Makiritare is the blowgun. It is about 3 meters long and consists of two concentric tubes. The inner tube is a notchless piece of Arundinaria, which (to prevent warping) is inserted into a stem of the paxiuba palm. To ensure a tight fit, the Indians coat the outside of the inner tube with a resinous adhesive. A conical mouthpiece carved from a fruit pit or a piece of suitable wood is fitted to one end of the blowgun and fastened with a curagua string. In rare cases a peccary tusk is fixed with resin to the tube some 30 centimeters from the mouthpiece to serve as a sight. The darts of the blowgun are 30 to 40 centimeters in length and 2 millimeters in diameter, usually made from the midrib of a seje palm leaf. A capoc wad is attached to the butt end of the dart, and 3 centimeters of the dart head are smeared with curare poison. A piranha tooth is used to notch the point so that it breaks off in the wound. Hunters retrieve these broken-off points from their kills and preserve them as trophies in the dart quivers. The quiver is made of a macanilla palm spath doubled over and sewn laterally with curagua fiber or cotton string. The 60-centimeter-long sheath is molded into shape by rubbing it with soft clay. For added reinforcement, the men wind curagua string in several turns along the entire length of the quiver at intervals of 4 to 5 centimeters, leaving an opening at one of the lateral seams near the top. Dangling from this opening are the piranha teeth used to sharpen and notch the darts. The hunter also carries a small rectangular pouch made of jaguar or deer skin to hold several other small implements and belongings necessary for the hunt or any other trip away from home. Into the pouch go his cartridges, fishhooks, onoto, small amulet rattles, and other things.

Several implements are needed to convert the raw and poisonous tuber of bitter yuca into manioc, the staple food of the Makiritare. Earlier we mentioned the yuca press, sieves, and carrying baskets. The yuca grater, essentially manufactured by the women, is so efficient that it has become a much-desired item of trade among the Guyana

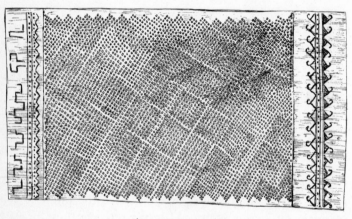

A yuca grater.

horticulturists. The man contributes the basic cedar board, approximately 140 centimeters long, 50 centimeters wide, and 2 centimeters thick, slightly planed convex-concave with axe and bush knife. The preliminary work accomplished, he hands over the board to his wife or daughter, who then commences the tedious task of inserting up to 3,000 minute triangular chips of quartz or jasper, which she has prepared and stored in a calabash.

For generations the Makiritare men have undertaken

annual expeditions to barter for the quartz and jasper or
to mine blocks of the crystal on a "jasper mountain" situated within their territory. Quarrying the mineral is laborious, transporting it is tedious, and its conversion by the
women into usable shards is extremely wasteful. No matter
how experienced the artisan, she strikes blow after blow
to produce the chips, of which but few have the desired
size and shape. During the last twenty years, however, small
pieces cut from tin cans have been used. In fact, these
metal points have almost replaced the mineral; discarded
tin cans are easier to obtain and are readily cut with a pair
of scissors into narrow strips and then into triangular
pieces of the proper size, which in turn can be quickly
inserted into the wooden base.

The insertion of the quartz or metal pieces into the surface is begun at the lower left corner or in the center and
continued in a pattern of intersecting diagonal lines previously diagramed on the board. The woman sits at her task
with the board placed lengthwise across her outstretched
legs, or she may raise the board on four short legs and sit
in front of it at the long side. She makes a little hole for
each chip by tapping the head of a nail with a hammer
stone or piece of bush knife. The same nail is also used to
press the chip deep into the groove. Gradually the woman
works the points into the entire surface, leaving only a
20-centimeter-wide border at the lower end of the grater,
and a somewhat narrower, unstudded border at the upper
end. The chips are set in a diagonal pattern so that the
grating action is most effective downward. Having inserted
the teeth of her grater, the woman will secure them further
by pouring several layers of rubber over the board, burying
the lower two-thirds of each chip and providing the wood
with a highly protective coating. She also uses the liquid
rubber to decorate the borders of the new grater with floral
and animal designs.

The importance of the dugout canoe to Makiritare life cannot be overestimated. Even the earliest accounts describe the Carib as highly mobile, expert navigators who undertook seasonal expeditions of considerable distance. Without the effective use of the dugout as a means of transportation, Carib warfare, trade, and territorial expansion, either in the distant past or, on a much reduced scale, in more recent times, are inconceivable. The Makiritare are excellent boat builders and their dugouts are highly prized as trade items by Creole and Indian neighbors alike. Cachicamo (palo maría), mure, and parature are among the local varieties of trees employed by the Makiritare for their boats. Initial shaping and excavation of the hull take place at the site where the tree was felled. Then the hull is carried or otherwise maneuvered to a place close to the settlement, where it is widened by fire and the finishing touches are added. In shallow waters, the boats are propelled by long poles; in deeper reaches, by paddles. Makiritare paddles have a crescent handle, a rounded shaft, and an oval blade. Sometimes the blade is shaped like a pointed shield with concave shoulders.

The Makiritare employ a relatively wide variety of musical instruments, both wind and percussion. Among wind instruments are flutes of bone and reed or wood. Made from the shinbone of the deer, a bone flute has three finger holes, is held in the vertical position, and is played by blowing across an aperture in the top. The lower third of the instrument is usually adorned with red cotton string twisted around the bone. Sometimes representations of monkeys and frogs are incised on the flute. There are two kinds of reed flutes. The simpler is a stopped, single end-blown flute made from a 50-centimeter-long piece of the same kind of Arundinaria reed that is used for the inner tube of the blowgun. The length of the air column is fixed by inserting a plug of beeswax. Besides the air hole on top

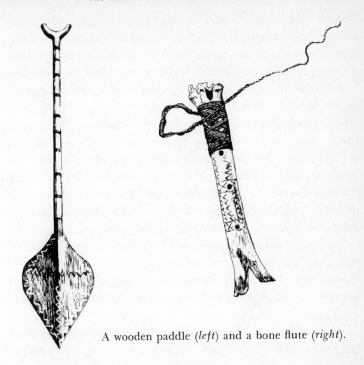

A wooden paddle *(left)* and a bone flute *(right)*.

of the instrument close to the mouthpiece, there are five finger holes distributed over the lower third of the flute and an additional hole on the back, diametrically opposite the uppermost finger hole. The entire surface of the flute is decorated with representations of frogs, fish, birds, monkeys, and abstract geometrical designs. This beautiful instrument is supposed to be capable of a range of three octaves. It certainly ranks among the finest wind instruments of indigenous Venezuela.

The second type of wooden flute is an open, three-hole end-blown flute, somewhat shorter than the stopped flute. Both ends are open, and the tone is produced by blowing against the upper rim of the tube.

Clarinets, used in pairs, one large (male) and one small

(female), are sacred musical instruments. These two symbolize a pair of mythical frogs and are always played in duet. The instruments are made from single pieces of bamboo, 1 to 1.5 meters long and 8 to 10 centimeters in diameter. Inserted in the top of the tube, close to the "mouthpiece," is the lamella, or reed, bound fast at one end to a base whose thickness determines the basic tone of the instrument. The "male" clarinet carries its lamella bound to a thicker base than the "female" and consequently produces a deeper sound. For the Makiritare listener, the music of the two clarinets is imitative of the dances of various types of birds and animals and is fraught with supernatural significance as accompaniment for ceremonial dances.

The large conch trumpet, opened at its apex, is an indispensable apotropaic instrument of the Makiritare. As among the Warao, it is blown to announce important events, the departures and arrivals of expeditions of men, traders, and warriors. Formerly the women in the settlement would answer the distant call on their own deer-skull trumpets. Nowadays conch shells are hard to find, and the cow-horn trumpet is occasionally used as a substitute.

There is a variety of percussion instruments in use among the Makiritare. Mention was made earlier of the rattle strings that the women, especially nubile girls, fasten to their loin cloths. A string of rattling fruit shells of a certain liana is also fastened to the top of a shamanic rattle staff, about 1.5 meters in length, which is used by the shaman primarily during the rites preceding his transport into a state of ecstasy. It is also used by the master of ceremonies at a dance, to direct the participants. The shaman makes use of a calabash rattle containing sacred stones and pieces of the roots of two special shamanic plants, one of which is known to be a hallucinogen when ingested. Red, blue, and white bird feathers (usually from the plumage of a woodpecker) decorate the top of the rattle stick. Another combination of colored plumage is red, yellow, and black. The handle of the shaman's rattle is beautifully carved with the figures of two celestial personages sitting back to back, elbows resting on their knees.

A fist rattle, made of a small calabash containing sacred stones and roots, is carried for protection by the Makiritare traveler. Should an evil force—a storm, malevolent shaman, a Kanaima spirit—approach him, he will take the rattle from its leather pouch, clench it in his fist, and thrust it repeatedly in the direction of the aggressor. The fist rattle has no pivotal central staff but is simply a small, closed resonance chamber. The stones and roots are inserted through a hole in the shell, which is then closed with resin. A similar amulet, containing the same protective agents as the fist rattle but much smaller in size, is worn by infants and young children on a neck string or tied to some other suitable body ornament. The pendant rattle emits a continuous soft rattling sound with every movement of the child. Another important instrument of the Makiritare is a cylindrical drum, some 45 to 60 centimeters deep and 35 to 50 centimeters in diameter. The drumhead is made of the skin of the jaguar, howler monkey, deer, or wild boar. Jaguar skin is preferred; that of the howler monkey ranks second. The drum is carried under one arm and beaten with a single stick. The music is a monotonous, slow beat to mark the rhythm of the steps for the ritual dance. The drummer may also choose to accompany his own recitation of the yuca festival or of the inauguration of a new communal dwelling.

The musical instruments of the Makiritare are closely associated with the religious elements of their life. It is therefore something of a surprise to see the drum used as accompaniment to the building of a house, an activity we would consider "secular." But the Makiritare look on the construction of a communal dwelling as an intrinsically religious act. In building a house, they are constructing a "temple," in which they will live in proximity to the supernatural world. In fact, it was the Supreme Being, Wanadi, himself who erected the first communal dwelling when he came to make his abode among the Makiritare. From this prototype the Indians acquired the proper proportions.

Prior to constructing a permanent house, especially the traditional round house, the elders of the group spend considerable time selecting a suitable site. The house must be built in a level clearing, close to good hunting grounds, and adjacent to a river. The water of the river must not be "acid" or cause diarrhea. The soil is examined for its suitability to nourish banana or yuca crops. Of course, the spirits of various plant species must not be offended; it is known that many of them will not tolerate humans in their vicinity. Storms arise from rocky areas, and so these, too, are to be avoided. The site of the communal house should not be too close to the settlements of the neighboring Yanoama. These and many other problems must be considered by the leaders before the communal house, the "center of the world," can rise majestically in the middle of the clearing.

Once the elders of the community have passed prudent judgment on the selection of a new dwelling site, the whole group, especially the male members, commence building the communal house, an activity that takes several months. Dimensions vary from house to house, but the length of the central pole determines the proportion of the other structural elements. The higher the central, pole, the greater the diameter of the house. Heights ranging from 8 to 16 meters have been recorded, with corresponding floor diameters of 15 to 30 meters. The massive conical roof of palm leaves rests on an outer ring of posts, which themselves serve as studs for the house wall of wattle-and-daub, concentric to the center pole. Between center pole and outer wall rises another concentric ring of supports made from even higher posts, the lower half of which support an inner wall of palm leaves, bark planks, or wattle-and-daub. The central area thus formed is reserved for the men—a circle with the center pole at the origin and an outer "ring of space" between its wall and the outer wall. Women are permitted to enter this inner living area of men and male adolescents only for the purpose of cleaning or to serve them their three daily meals, which must be done in strict silence.

The central area functions as common room, dining room, and dormitory for the unwed males of the group, as well as for male guests. When the occasion arises, the area is used as a dance floor for religious ceremonies. It is also the place where the shaman, seated on his jaguar bench beside the center pole, undertakes the curing of the sick. The concentric ring between inner and outer wall is compartmentalized into three or four major sections, separated from each other by bark panel walls. Each compartment houses an extended family. There is a door connecting each compartment with the central area which is used by the women and their nubile daughters strictly as a service entrance.

The outer wall of the communal dwelling is approximately 1.7 meters high. On the east side of the wall is an opening which serves as main entrance, from which a corridor leads directly to the central area. Minor entrances, each opening into a family compartment, are found at three or more locations in the outer wall—one entrance from the outside to each compartment, each with a door made of a solid wooden slab. Oriented in a northwest direction is a skylight in the roof. This rectangular window section of the roof turns on two lateral hinges located on the median line and is operated from the central area by means of a rawhide pull.

The communal house represents a miniature of the Makiritare macrocosmos. The roof is the heavenly vault supported by a major cross-beam—the Milky Way. The central pole is the *axis mundi,* the axis of rotation for the celestial dome. The shaman sits at the foot of the center pole, the center of the universe. From this point, he "ascends" the world axis through eight successive heavens (each of which is marked off with onoto on the central pole) to reach the world of Wanadi above. The Sacred Monkey made a similar ascent when he went to acquire the first bitter yuca for the Makiritare. In reality, the communal house is the cosmic center of the universe for the Makiritare. Here they dwell under the protection of Wanadi, in the shadow of the (yuca) world tree, which grows next to the central pole at the point where the heavens touch the earth.

Inside the house, located on the outer wall, are the fireplaces. Raised platforms, accessible by notched logs, provide storage space. Hammocks, often slung one above the other, serve as beds at night and as seats during working hours. Originally the shaman's jaguar bench was used ex-

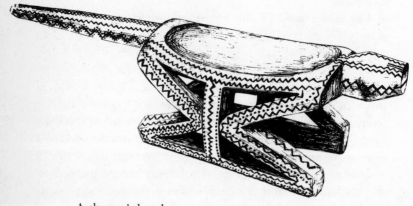

A shaman's bench.

clusively for ceremonial purposes, but nowadays it is also
used by men other than the shamans. The jaguar bench is
an oval, concave seat carved from a single block of wood,
stained red with onoto, and decorated with black designs
along all the edges.

Usually a large communal house provides shelter for an
entire local group, numbering between 50 and 120 individuals. The house is deserted following the death of its
chief or shaman and is temporarily abandoned if a group
of one or more extended families embarks on a fishing trip
of several months' duration. In either circumstance, the
Makiritare construct a less complete dwelling, called
homakari, a rectangular structure with a saddle roof semi-
conically rounded at each end. The relatively low walls are
made of juxtaposed poles or palm leaves or mold. Windows
are rare. Individual family compartments are separated by
walls made of bark panels. The semicircular areas at each
end are reserved for the men. Depending on the number
of family compartments necessary, the homakari may have
a length of up to 30 meters and a width of 8 meters. The
saddle-roofed rectangular house type is gradually replacing
the communal dwelling of circular cross-section. A local
group may occupy three to six of these houses, depending
on how many extended families constitute the settlement.

When the settlement consists of a number of such rectangular dwellings, one of them is always reserved for the
exclusive use of the men. In this case the semicircular
space at each end of the rectangular dwelling functions as
working area, for the preparation of cassava, for instance.
Rectangular houses of the homakari type among the
Makiritare and other Carib tribes have traditionally been
used as worksheds and as hostels for foreign visitors, especially whites. The use of such smaller houses by single
nuclear families of Makiritare on the Caura, Ventuari, and

Cunucunuma rivers is a direct consequence of mission influence.

The most provisional kind of shelter used by the Makiritare is constructed for a group on the march. Four to six posts are cut and set to support the roof, which slants down from front to back. Such a hut can accommodate the hammocks of up to a dozen people, although the platanillo covering of the roof dries rapidly and cracks open after a few days. A similar type of open shelter, but longer and sturdier, is erected to house the members of a community when they are away from the settlement on a major hunting expedition. The chief occupies the center, and a central portion of the hut is reserved for the men alone. Such temporary huts are quickly put together when the traveling party steps ashore shortly before sunset; in half an hour the roof is ready. The small ones are not intended to last more than one or two nights; hunting expeditions can make do in the larger shelters for several weeks.

FOOD-QUEST ACTIVITIES

The two main pillars of Makiritare economy are horticulture and hunting. Rather surprisingly, considering their familiarity with the rivers and their skill as boatmen, fishing is of secondary importance. No Makiritare feels that he has truly eaten unless his meal has consisted of a generous helping of cassava and of meat.

Horticulture is woman's work; the men clear the forest land. The clearing activity is planned by the chief and elders after each family has made known its preference for field location. Toward the end of the rainy season, the whole community becomes involved. Singing, the men attack the forest with their axes, the din punctuated by euphoric shouts as the trees come crashing down. Adolescent boys carry the drums, while beautifully attired girls hand out copious amounts of yaraki beer. Small children

climb among the fallen trees to distribute fresh cigars to
the workers. The best of Makiritare cuisine is served in the
early afternoon by the women, right on the virgin clearing.
Two months later enormous bonfires will devour the dried
vegetation on the same clearing, and then the women will
set the first seedlings into the still-warm soil. Only mothers
and their adolescent daughters may plant; the fields are
taboo for sterile women because a correlation exists between the fertility of soil and that of women. Each of the
various fields is planted in turn, one after the other, by all
the women. The harvest of each field, however, is specifically the property of the family with whom it is initially
identified.

Bitter yuca, the staple crop of the Makiritare, is planted
in great quantities. Settings are also made of plantains,
bananas, sweet potatoes, sweet yuca, mapuey, ocumo, yams,
maize, sugar cane, pineapples, papaya, peppers, and tobacco. Arrowgrass and calabash are also cultivated, as well
as several medicinal and "magic" plants.

The root of the bitter yuca cannot be eaten before the
hydrocyanic (prussic) acid it contains has been totally extracted, a laborious process that occupies the women for
many hours each day. The women first pick the tubers,
then clean and peel them, then reduce them to a white
pulp on yuca graters. The pulp is collected in a section of
discarded canoe, and large quantities are packed into the
basketry yuca presses. A full press is so heavy that two
women are needed to carry it to a special scaffold. Here
the press is hung high from an upper beam. A pole lever is
passed through the lower loop on the press and the end
secured to a fixed point. The long arm of the lever is
pressed down and slipped into the uppermost of a series
of angular cuts on a pole driven deep into the ground at
an appropriate distance from the suspended press. The
liquid seeps through the bottom of the basketry press

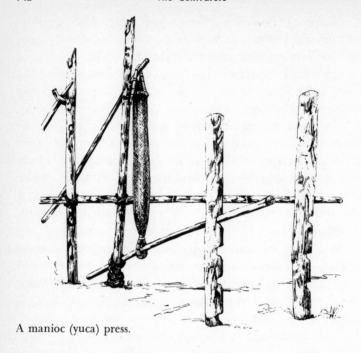

A manioc (yuca) press.

under pressure, which is increased from time to time by pushing the lever down another notch. Most of the poisonous acid is removed in the fluid pressed out from the pulp. Finally, the press is taken down and the damp white flour extracted. The pressure exerted on the mass within the yuca press is so great that the compressed pulp comes out in two or three long solid columns, as white as plaster of paris. This must then be broken up, pulverized, and strained through a basketry sieve before it can be used.

Some of the resulting flour is made into soup. The major portion, however, is baked on a large round iron or clay slab in thin cassava "tortillas" as big as cartwheels. Baking is accomplished over a slow fire, with the iron grid resting on several stones. The large, baked "tortillas" are often placed on the roof to dry in the sun. Large quantities of yuca flour are also toasted on special pans and processed into mandioca. Mandioca is packed into mapire baskets lined with platanillo leaves and covered with the same kind of leaves to keep the humidity out. The Makiritare take several of these full baskets along on extended expeditions. An open basket rests next to the man paddling the boat, so that whenever he is hungry he can take a fistful of mandioca, dunk it in the river, and eat it.

Sweet potatoes, mapuey, yams, and ocumo are planted in small quantities only and are consumed exclusively in a thick soup at the end of a meal. Maize has only recently been adopted and is still rare. The green ears are roasted and eaten between meals. Sugar cane is relatively abundant and is sucked out mostly by the women and children.

Hunting and fishing are men's work. The shotgun and curare-tipped arrows are used mainly for hunting tapir, deer, peccary, anteaters, male alligators, armadillos, and turtles. Chiguire, dolphins, snakes, agouti, and paca are not food animals; nor is the monkey, except during hard times, and then only men may eat of its flesh.

The blowgun is used exclusively for small game and such birds as turkeys, toucans, gallineta, and parrots. The hunter usually leaves the house before sunrise. He waits for the first bird calls as light dawns, makes his kill, and returns to the house in the early morning hours. A young man will often take his wife along on such outings. The successful hunter plucks the tail feathers from the bird and hangs them from the branch of a tree near the spot where it died. This practice ensures his future luck and, at the same time, guarantees continued abundance.

The battue, or drive, is one of the two major Makiritare hunting techniques. Preparations commence when fresh tracks are sighted, for all the menfolk of the settlement will participate. The women prepare a lotion of water and a certain liana to wash the feet of their men as a protective

measure against snakebite. For the same purpose they also
paint the feet of the men with onoto. The torso and face
of the hunter are decorated in geometrical designs. The
shamans ascertain that a piece of fresh-water dolphin jaw-
bone will be taken along by the hunters, and that each has
his fist rattle for the chase. Finally, the hunters and their
dogs leave in family groups. They paddle to the location of
the tracks, moor the boats, and enter the forest.

The purpose of the Makiritare chase is to drive the
animals out of the forest into the river, at the point where
some of the men are waiting in the boats. To track the animals down and flush them to the river takes the better part
of a day, and the hunters persist, never deviating from the
original track, even though newer, fresher spore be found.
Sighted birds are shot if such momentary digression requires no deviation from the track of the animal pursued.
Makiritare hunters are superior trackers, following the
animal at a jog for hours. The pace accelerates once the
track becomes quite fresh or warm excrement is discovered,
or as soon as the hunting dogs pick up the scent of the
fleeing game. Once the animals are overtaken and turned
back toward the river, the hunters spread out in a line
arching back to embrace as much as 5 kilometers of open
river front between the terminal points of the beat. The
men on the river, meanwhile, have spaced themselves
strategically in their boats along the shore and shoot or
stab the panicked animals as they enter the water to escape
the frenzied dogs.

Large packs of dogs are taken along for such a hunt; a
single family may bring as many as twenty. They are indispensable for flushing the animals from their hiding
places, for keeping them moving once the chase back to
the river has begun, and for holding individual animals at
bay in a thicket or morass until the hunter arrives to make
the kill. Should the dogs allow an animal to escape, the

Makiritare attribute the loss to adverse influences caused by the shaman. The loss of a dog's hunting prowess is irreparable. Furthermore, if a dog fails to hold an animal because it has licked menstrual blood, it must be "purified," in a way that almost asphyxiates the beast. The head of the dog is held in the ventilation hole of an earthen oven, and the animal is made to inhale thick, acrid fumes from smoldering green wood and pieces of fur from larger game, or vapors from a generous quantity of pounded, toasted peppers sprinkled over the coals.

Before the catch is loaded onto the boats, each of the animals killed is inspected by the leader of the group that made the beat to ascertain that it is of a commonly recognized species and free of deformity. If the game is killed in the forest far away from the settlement, the hunters disembowel the carcass, submerge it in the shallow waters of a nearby rivulet, and carry the intestines home to be prepared and eaten. The next day several women accompany one of the hunters to quarter the carcass and pack it back to the entrance of the village. Here they wait for an elder of the tribe to come forth with a whip. Each receives several lashes across the lower trunk and the legs. Only then may the meat be carried into the settlement for the chief to mark the portion allotted to each family. The size of the portions varies according to respective family size. The women carry the allotments to the different family hearths and return to their quarters. Children may not eat the meat of peccary, chácharo, or anteater. Men observing taboo restrictions following the birth of one of their children (couvade) must also abstain.

The second major Makiritare hunting practice is the extended expedition lasting for weeks or even months. The whole village abandons the communal house with its surrounding fields and plunges euphorically into a Paleo-Indian life of camping, hunting, and gathering. The families take to canoes for a two or three days' journey from the village. After the canoes are beached, a rectangular shed-like shelter is erected for all, from which base the men sally forth each day at sunrise to hunt a predetermined area. The efforts of the day yield dozens of pieces of game, which are packed in as the sun sets, so that the roasting grills at the camp site are literally smothered in chunks of meat piled one upon another. Twice daily, early in the morning and again late at night, the Indians gorge themselves on great quantities of meat. The rest of the kill is smoke-dried and preserved for leaner days. The daily hunts continue until the area has been depleted of game, at which point the community returns to the permanent settlement, eager now for a change of diet.

While the men are out every day on the hunt, the women try their hand at fishing with hook and line. They also accompany their men on fishing trips, which commence in the afternoon. Either a fishline is dropped from the boat, or they pause in a lagoon for the man to shoot the fish with harpoon arrows fired from a special fishing bow. Strong hooks are also baited for the large aymara and left tied to low branches along the river bank at night.

Another technique is the use of piscides. Fishing with barbasco is a family affair. The roots of a particular liana are crushed on a tree trunk or another hard surface and gathered into fibrous balls, which are stored in one or two canoes. When some forty to sixty such crushed root balls are collected they are washed overboard and the milky juice spreads throughout the rivulet. The smaller fish are stunned and are easily scooped out with landing nets by all —men, women, and children. Struggling for oxygen, the larger fish surface and are shot with harpoon arrows. Fires are lit, and the entire group settles to eat the fresh catch while the surplus is smoked for future consumption. Barbasco fishing carries several taboos: no river may be fished more than once within a given year, and all who participate must abstain from sexual intercourse for some time. Certain fish are taboo for children, and men observing the couvade may not eat piranha, the fat katishi, and certain other species.

The collecting of wild edibles is minimal among the Makiritare. The Indians delight, however, in a species of long earthworm, a certain type of leafcutter ant, the larvae of palm beetles, turtle eggs, and frogs. The fruits of the seje, cucurito, coroba, pijiguao, yagrumo, and several other wild vegetables are collected seasonally. The palm cabbage of the cucurito and manaca are also greatly appreciated.

The Makiritare keep no domesticated animals other than dogs and chickens, neither of which is ever eaten. In fact, even the eggs of chickens are traditionally not consumed.

The Indians rarely drink plain water, preferring any of three unfermented beverages, called yucuta. They also have two alcoholic varieties of drink, known as yaraki. One kind of yucuta is made from fresh yuca flour mixed with water, usually served cold, except during the rainy season, when it is heated and served warm after breakfast. Another yucuta consists of toasted manioc flour mixed with water. The third type is made of bananas added to fresh yuca-flour yucuta; the creamy result is served hot as a breakfast drink during the rainy season. Seasonally the Makiritare enjoy the juice of the fruit of the seje and the cucurito palms. Sugar cane juice is also a great treat. Alcoholic beverages are brewed in huge, hollow-log troughs. The common yaraki is a fermented drink made from bitter yuca, with either the decomposed tubers or yuca mash used as a base to which certain herbs are sometimes added for flavor. Aged for several days, the drink takes on a tangy, acid taste, and this is the yuca beer preferred by the men. The second kind of yaraki is a fermented brew made from a base of sweet yuca and potato mash. This, the favorite drink of the women and children, must be consumed during the early stage of fermentation, for it becomes increasingly toxic as it ages.

Both men and women smoke tobacco rolled into big cigars of bast or leaves from the ears of maize. Etiquette requires that a gift of cigars be offered to a guest by the members of the community as a gesture of friendship. Shamans grow a particularly strong type of tobacco for their personal use, and the hallucinogenic root mentioned earlier is smoked for shamanistic purposes only.

In earlier days the Makiritare produced fire by the rotation method, whereby one stick (for example, of the onoto tree) is twirled vertically in a notch carved in a second stick held firmly horizontal on the ground. Now the In-

A cigar holder (*left*), used by the shaman, and a ceremonial club (*right*).

Makiritare of the Upper Ventuari River constructing a communal house.

The first step in the process of making a dugout canoe: felling the selected tree.

3

Makiritare of the Erebato
River fabricating a
cotton hammock.

A Makiritare woman
tending her triangular
roasting grill
packed with meat.

Supported by a
hanging chair, a
Makiritare baby
practices his
first steps.

5

Makiritare mother
and child.

6

7

A young Makiritare couple from the Upper Caura River region dressing for a festive occasion.

Makiritare from the Upper Caura River region dance to the music of sacred clarinets and a drum.

dians rarely have to resort to the indigenous method, however, for matches are more or less constantly available. Illumination within the house is provided by torches made of resin wrapped in palm leaf and tied with lianas.

Much of the vegetable and protein food collected—for example, fruits, palmito, larvae, and turtle eggs—is eaten raw. Most foods, however, are boiled or roasted. Boiled meat is usually heavily seasoned with peppers. On special occasions, ground roasted peppers mixed in equal parts with salt, or boiled peppers cured with aromatic herbs and acid termites, are added to spice a special dish. Peppers boiled with fresh yuca flour or with yari provide a spicy sauce to make the cassava more palatable during the rainy season, when meat and fish are scarce and the endless cassava dunked in kümawi sauces becomes a monotonous diet. (Yari is the creamy, sweet residue remaining in the pot after the poisonous juices extracted from the raw, bitter yuca pulp in the press have boiled away. The prussic acid is eliminated in this lengthy process.) The oil of seje palm is the only cooking oil found in the Makiritare kitchen. Fish and meat are roasted on a tripod grill. Living far away from any source of salt, either natural or commercially prepared, the Makiritare probably used to satisfy their minimal needs with the surrogate salt in the seared exterior of roasted meat. Salt has always been a highly desirable trade item. It is said that the Caribs have even waged wars against tribes more privileged in their access to this commodity.

SOCIAL ORGANIZATION

Though characterized by a common language and a shared culture, and enjoying close intergroup relationships, the three major regional Makiritare subgroups in the Caura, Ventuari, and Cunucunuma river basins do not recognize either a paramount chief or regional government, and thus lack political unity on either a regional or a tribal level. Each of the thirty-odd local groups follows the direction of a village chief, whose "commands" rarely amount to more than pronouncements of the consensus of opinion proceeding from the council of adult men. The office of chief is not hereditary, and in circumstances that require special expertise, such as leadership in time of war, trading expeditions, and negotiations with whites, the chief is quick to recognize the authority of some tribesman better qualified than himself. The members of a residential group display considerable *esprit de corps*, because the effective social organization to which an individual belongs never overrides the nuclear family within the extended family of the group or band.

The social structure of the Makiritare corresponds to what has become known as the "Carib type" of cognatic system. That is, their quasi-unilineal social organization characteristically de-emphasizes small domestic units in favor of a more prominent, large, extended family. The nuclear family is, of course, recognizable as an operative unit among the Makiritare but its singular independence is shrouded by the interdependence of the several nuclear families within the extended family and the band.

Makiritare descent is reckoned matrilineally; after marriage the groom goes to live with the family of his wife. First-cousin marriage is allowed, provided that the contracting partners are cross-cousins (father's sisters' or mother's brothers' children). The Makiritare, in fact, consider cross-cousin marriage most practical, for the spouses have known each other for years, and the bonds of friendship between their families become reinforced through the bonds of marriage between them. As a result, marriageable boys and girls are often living within the same residential unit, so that the local group tends to be a predominantly endogamous kin group. A strong matri-bias prevails among the

Makiritare, as among other Venezuelan Caribs, but characteristically any such unilineal principle remains subordinate to the cognatic system.

Polygyny is practiced by many Makiritare men, who may be married at any given time to from two to five women, and sororal marriages are frequent. The levirate is practiced in the event that the deceased husband's brother is a bachelor. Although polygyny is usually practiced only by the elders of the tribe, it does not seem to signify higher status or rank. The incest taboo does not apply to second cousins and nieces. In accordance with the cross-cousin marriage rule, the kinship system is of the Iroquois type; the avuncular terminology is bifurcate merging.

The Makiritare have had strained relations with the Yanoama for more than a hundred years, and these have often flared into open hostilities. In the early eighteenth century the Makiritare were forced to evacuate their southern territories. Even in the present century, several Makiritare villages had to pool their resources to repel a major Yanoama attack. Under siege, the communal hut becomes a fortress, and firearms are the only real hope for the survival of the harassed few in the settlement. Witness an apprehensive group of Makiritare sleeping with rifles under their hammocks as they travel through Yanoama frontierland today, and recall the bold Carib raiding parties of centuries past, when the tribes were aggressive, fierce, and numerous. Probably the dwindling Makiritare population would have succumbed completely to the Yanoama had it not been for their possession of firearms, not to mention the fact that the Yanoama greatly desired the indigenous and exotic trade goods to which only the Makiritare had access. Today the Makiritare and the Yanoama live in more or less friendly symbiosis along the frontier. Occasionally Makiritare men have taken Yanoama women, who adapt relatively successfully to the tribal customs and mores of their husbands. Because of their Neo-Indian level of cultural achievement, all Makiritare consider themselves vastly superior to the Yanoama.

LIFE CYCLE AND RELIGIOUS BELIEFS

The more intimate activities of the Makiritare are relatively simple. Sex play among children is common, and masturbation by both boys and girls is condoned. After reaching puberty, girls have complete sexual freedom, and the offspring resulting from premarital intercourse are completely accepted, for there are no social sanctions against such occurrences. But if paternity cannot be established conclusively, the mother will kill the infant for fear that it is the offspring of a spirit. Generally sexual intercourse, even between spouses, takes place in the privacy of the forest, when the couple is engaged in the daily routine of hunting and foraging.

Certain food taboos are observed by both parents before the birth of a child, and sexual intercourse is discontinued during the last months of pregnancy lest physical harm be done to the fetus. Abstinence from the flesh of certain animals is also observed during the period of gestation, lest certain undesirable characteristics of the animals be magically transferred to the child within the womb.

Birth takes place in the family room of the communal house. The woman kneels in front of her hammock with her arms behind her, holding onto the net. During the final stage of labor, experienced old women assist by massaging the mother's abdomen. If need be, they will send for the shaman to alleviate the pain by blowing tobacco smoke over the abdomen and back of the mother. All other men are banned from the scene of the birth. After the birth of the child, both parents are restricted to certain foods, and further couvade prohibitions severely limit their activities. The father may not go out to hunt or touch metal tools or weapons of any kind. Deformed babies are abandoned or killed, as is one member of a set of twins. A stillbirth is thought to be the result of a curse cast on the woman by a tribesman.

Soon after birth the child is formally presented to the members of the community, who come to pay their respects to the new infant and his parents in the family compound. At about the time when the umbilical cord has dried and fallen off, a purification ceremony takes place. Old and young maternal kin of the newborn listen for several hours to the song of the shaman and then form a procession to the river. At the bank the maternal grandfather sits in a boat facing the river, smoking two cigars simultaneously as he sings songs of exorcism in unison with the shaman. Both men interrupt their chant twice to blow ritually over a calabash brought by the grandmother, containing water, herbs, and fragrant pieces of wood. When the singing finally ceases, the maternal grandfather pours water from the calabash through a sieve over the baby held in the mother's arms. Then the grandmother takes the infant and comforts it while the mother is washed by the old man, her father, with water poured from the calabash through the basketry sieve. The mother removes and washes her loincloth and then her whole body. Cradling her child once more in her arms, she takes the seat in the boat formerly occupied by her father. He stands beside her in the boat and blows over the head of his daughter. Both grandfather and shaman then spit into the water on both sides of the boat as well as in the direction of the spot where they had earlier thrown the firebrands from which the ceremonial cigars had been lit. Next the father of the child pours the remainder of the water in the calabash over his own feet. Subsequently the entire group returns to the village to hear a kinsman of the infant announce formally: "It's a boy!" or, "It's a girl!" With his formal presentation to society, the infant becomes a recognized member of the local group. The grandparents give him a name: a nickname of animal derivation, one descriptive of some body characteristic, or a name of Spanish origin. The Makiritare, like so many indigenous tribes, are reluctant to reveal their names, for they consider them extremely private. Kinfolk call one another by the appropriate kinship term instead, although this custom is gradually being replaced by Spanish names.

Wherever she goes, a Makiritare mother takes her infant child in a baby sling or held on the hip. The children are breast-fed until the age of three. Grandparents and elder siblings are often called upon to babysit, and all are very permissive. In general, the socialization process is set by the pace of the child's own individual development rather than by adherence to and reinforcement of an arbitrary set of competitive norms and rules. Fathers teach their sons the arts of a man's domain and the mothers impart their domestic knowledge to their daughters.

At puberty both sexes undergo initiation ceremonies. In times past, boys coming of age were ceremonially whipped and subjected to the well-known ant ordeal, in which huge biting ants, imprisoned in a basketry frame, are set upon the arms and trunk of the initiate. The ordeal is also part of the hunting-magic complex; from time to time grown men undergo the same test of pain. Nowadays this ant ordeal is no longer practiced.

When menstruation comes to a girl for the first time, she is secluded in the family quarters of the communal dwelling for a period of two or three weeks. During this time she remains silent and may eat but little, and then only food that the shaman has "blown upon." She may not cook for the men, although women may eat the food she prepares without coming to harm. When the period of seclusion has come to an end, she is led by the women to the fields, where she engages symbolically in various planting and harvesting activities. This done, she sets out for home once more, running a specially prepared obstacle course over thorn bushes and rope traps—finally to pass by the crudely carved figure of "a man who looks on her." She flies over the trail as fast as she can, for she is pursued by a horde of men and women seeking to catch and whip her. Six months later, the frontal hair of the girl is shorn while the headman sings, she repeating the instructional chants after him. When this hair has grown again, the girl is given a haircut typical of Makiritare adult women. From this moment the young woman is recognized as ready for marriage, and she expects her parents to select a spouse for her sooner or later.

Love and personal inclination toward a particular individual have been traditionally subordinated to more practical considerations, but lately such feelings are taken more into account in the choice of a spouse. Once the parents have reached agreement, the groom arranges to meet his bride in the family compound of her parents. His in-laws leave the house for this occasion so that the bride may meet the groom alone. She offers him a calabash of yucuta, then drinks from the same cup. The calabash is emptied in this ceremonial exchange, and the couple then look upon each other as man and wife. The young man has brought wedding presents for his parents-in-law: gunpowder or tools for the father of the bride, cotton cloth for her mother. He is not expected to render bride-service. After the private marriage ceremony, the couple usually leaves the settlement to spend the initial days of married life alone, away from the distracting noise of the villagers.

Early marriage for girls is the rule, and there are virtually no bachelors. Divorce, when it occurs, is relatively

easy to obtain on such grounds as infidelity, laziness, or
refusal to bear children. Small children remain with the
mother, although adolescent boys may subsequently choose
to live with their father. If a woman is deserted by a
vagrant husband, she will soon join another man in marriage. The social customs of the tribe are generally so
flexible that any catastrophic emotional scene between the
marriage partners is quite unnecessary should either of
them desire divorce. But, as a rule, Makiritare couples live
in harmony, caring for each other and for their offspring
with great affection.

The adults share the daily burden of living, each performing the duties assigned to his sex. The woman tends
the house and children and works in the field; the man
clears a piece of the forest, performing the food-quest
activities of hunting and fishing, builds canoes and houses,
and goes on prolonged trading expeditions.

Makiritare adults observe avoidance taboos with regard
to parents-in-law—especially those of the opposite sex.
This puts a strain on the bridegroom, who, according to
the rule of matrilocal residence, lives under the same roof
with his mother-in-law. But the avoidance taboo is less
restrictive if the man's mother-in-law is also his own aunt.
Thus cross-cousin marriage carries an advantage in addition to those mentioned earlier. Despite the deep mutual
understanding that characterizes the Makiritare couple,
both men and women are very reserved and are reluctant
to demonstrate their affection in public, to the degree that
they will not even address each other in the presence of
others.

The Makiritare Indians believe in a three-level cosmos:
heaven, earth, and the underworld. Heaven has eight
strata, one upon another; earth is earth; the underworld
has three strata. Earth is connected with the eight-layered
heaven by a central pole, associated with a host of details

reminiscent of the "Tree of Life" complex. The upper-most stratum of heaven is inhabited by Wanadi (the Supreme Being, son of the Sun), by Wanadi's family, and by those ancestor spirits who are fortunate enough to reach Wanadi's world after traversing the seven inferior heavenly strata. Wanadi is the transcendent god who created animal, plant, and human life on earth. He is also the benevolent spirit with whom a person may converse and to whom offerings of food are made. A shaman "visits" Wanadi to receive the jaguar bench, the sacred rattle, and the celestial quartz crystals.

The Indians tell of a chain of very powerful and benevolent shamans who lived in times long past. In those days there was no evil on the earth. Evil entered the land of the Makiritare and into their very lives with the advent of trading for iron tools with the Cariban tribes to the east. Shamanistic power, the gift of Wanadi, was then usurped by perverted men who turned against their own people. One of these evil shamans, Kanaima, killed his fellow men and finally took his own life. His son rubbed the father's blood all over his body, transformed himself into a jaguar, and from that moment subsisted solely on the blood of his human victims. Today the number of jaguar, vampire, and serpent Kanaimas is legion. All of them seek out men to kill, especially men who wander alone, to suck their blood for nourishment. The shaman is the preserver of the vital energy of the soul of each individual and of the group. Through his ingestion of certain psychedelic plants, the shaman attains the ability to illumine the interior of a person, to determine the state of his soul. The same drugs also enable him to find his way through the dark underworld in his search for lost souls.

Tobacco and hallucinogens are similarly instrumental in the formation of the neophyte shaman, whose ritual "death" is brought about through the copious use of psychotropic and narcotic agents. Unconscious, or sunk in a deep trance, the young man's body "frees" his soul to soar through the various heavens to the land of Wanadi. His revival is achieved through a bath in "celestial waters of eternal youth," and on his return he intones the shamanistic song in a ceremonial language unintelligible to laymen. He brings back the sacred quartz crystals for his shaman's rattle, and from the moment of his return to the land of the living he is a different person, who keeps to himself, apart from the rest of the men and from the group. The quartz crystals are said to be the spirits of deceased shamans.

Shamans are called upon to cure illnesses proceeding from any of three scourges. The first is the introduction of an evil substance by a malevolent shaman, by one of the Kanaima demons, by the spirit of a beast killed by the father of an ailing child, by the overwhelming charge of vital energy experienced by the invalid's progenitor in moments of danger, or by the vagrant soul of a defunct person. To rid the victim of such an illness, the shaman calls upon Wanadi and a host of mythical heroes. The chants, the heavy tobacco smoke, and the quartz pieces in his rattle are powerful aids. Sick children suffering a deficiency of vital energy for the reasons mentioned receive the healing breath of the shaman directly on the mouth. The shaman may also be able to detect a materialization of the vital energy of the beast killed by the father of the young patient, in which case he "extracts" with his hand from the chest of the child a small piece of bone or skin of the animal concerned. The disabling poison introduced into a victim by a malevolent shaman may be either magical or nonmagical. The real poison is derived from the root of woí, a plant grown for this purpose in the fields, mixed with the victim's food, and used mainly for personal vendettas. Poison can also be sent by a malevolent shaman from a neighboring tribe and is believed to produce many serious illnesses. An antidote for this magically produced suffering can be prepared by a friendly shaman or another male member of the tribe. The curer usually boils the woí root, adds some blood drawn from the patient, boils the mixture for several hours, and then pours it all out on the ground and into the fire. Should the patient die nonetheless, the shaman may cut off a finger of the victim and boil it with bits of woí root to bring about the death of the distant assassin.

The second cause of sickness is a transgression of the moral or ethical code of the tribe. A proper confession and propitiatory gifts made to the shaman can effect a cure, but only subsequent observance of the cultural taboos can bring about full restoration of health.

The third cause of illness is soul loss. Soul loss can occur from bad dreams, through theft by a shaman or evil spirit, or through capture by the Moon. The shaman embarks on an ecstatic journey to retrieve the lost soul and return it to his suffering patient. When an Indian dies, the Moon seeks to intercept his soul on its ascent to heaven. Here again, the shaman, as psychopomp, or spirit guide, recovers the soul and directs it along the route to heaven. He alone knows how to pass through a perilous passage of rapidly opening and closing scissors that obstructs the road, and he alone is sufficiently experienced to resist the allurements of a siren-like temptress, who kills any suitor she succeeds in embracing.

Some foodstuffs, especially "heavy" meat like that of the tapir, can be eaten only by the weaker members of the tribe—children, young men, and young women—subsequent to their submission to ritual whipping. Sick people must abstain completely from such meat and are allowed only "light" foods, such as fish and the flesh of rodents, in order to prevent the exacerbation of the illness.

Pathogens are transferable even after death. Therefore a corpse is sometimes cremated, and those—especially the close kin of the deceased—who handle the dead must live in isolation from the rest of the tribe for one full year, avoid eating "heavy" foods, and observe a series of additional taboos. The tools used by the dead in this life, together with all the implements employed in the disposal of the corpse, become dangerously contaminated and must be discarded.

Whenever possible, a terminally ill individual is left to die outside the communal dwelling, so that he may be interred in a canoe some distance away from the house. Should he die within the house, he is buried directly beneath the spot where his hammock used to hang in the family compound. Should multiple deaths occur, as is often the case during an epidemic, the dead are buried in the house and the whole structure is burned to the ground. The same applies on the occasion of the death of a chief. A respected shaman is sometimes afforded secondary burial in order that the community may benefit from his protection even after his demise. The corpse is dried on a platform in the open air and the bones recovered are kept in the house by the surviving wives or other female relatives. Before disposing of the dead, the women commence their wailing in the prescribed manner, the right elbow resting on the knee and the face covered with the hand. A second wailing takes place several weeks or even months later, on the occasion of the first meeting of the kinswomen of the defunct, or when close kinsmen of both sexes reunite after a prolonged period of separation. The vital essence of a dead Makiritare remains close to his earthly remains at the burial place, while his soul either ascends to heaven or descends to the underworld.

Besides his functions as curer and psychopomp, the shaman maintains ceaseless vigil over his fellow men, lest any breach of conduct upset the equilibrium of the group or any failure to observe the many restrictive taboos endanger the entire society. It is he who will ensure an abundance of game and fish, and only he holds sway over the adverse elements of nature. In addition, he interprets events of the past and divines those of the future.

As mentioned, the shaman effects cures and contacts the supernatural world while seated at the foot of the central pole of the house. A curing ceremony starts some time after sunset and lasts for several hours. The inhabitants of the house maintain a vigil with the shaman and his patient and are witness to the traffic along the central pole between the religious practitioner and the metaphysical forces. The patient (or patients) is seated in front of the shaman with his back to him. The shaman cures by chanting, fumigating with tobacco smoke, massaging the afflicted parts of the body, blowing, and shaking his rattle. In a demonstration fraught with ecstatic emotion, he identifies and finally extracts the sickness through sucking and the use of his rattle.

Shamans are paid for their services, and their privileged position on earth is carried over after death, for they are converted into stars and live forever in the seventh heavenly stratum, in close proximity to Wanadi. In the past, the shaman fulfilled a sublime function as intermediary between his people and the supernatural. Nowadays, there are no great shamans left among the Makiritare, because of the advance of the frontier in general and the influence of the missions in particular. When the last communal house was abandoned, the last visible world axis was relinquished, and the last full-fledged shaman took the cosmic image of the Makiritare with him to his grave.

162 *The Cultivators*

BIBLIOGRAPHY

Barandiarán, Daniel de, "Actividades Vitales de Subsistencia de los Indios Yecuana o Makiritare," *Antropológica*, No. 11 (1962a), 1-29.

———, "Shamanismo Yecuana o Makiritare," *Antropológica*, No. 11 (1962b), 61-90.

———, "El Habitado entre los Indios Yecuana," *Antropológica*, No. 16 (1966), 1-95.

———, "Cultura Material de los Indios Yecuana." Manuscript.

Civrieux, Marc de, "Datos Antropológicas de los Indios Kunuhana," *Antropológica*, No. 8 (1959), 85-146.

———, *Watunna. Mitología Makiritare.* Caracas: 1970.

Coppens, Walter, "A Makiritare Village in Transition." Manuscript.

Fuchs, Helmuth, "La Estructura Residencial de los Maquiritare de 'El Corobal' y 'Las Ceibas,' Territoria Federal Amazonas, Venezuela," *América Indígena*, XXII, No. 2 (1962), 169-90.

———, "El Sistema de Cultivo de los Deukwhuana (Maquiritare) del Alto Río Ventuari, Terrritorio Federal Amazonas, Venezuela," *América Indígena*, XXIV, No. 2 (1964), 171-95.

Koch-Grünberg, Theodor, "Vom Roraima zum Orinoco." *Ethnographie*, III. Stuttgart: 1923.

Ocando-Orio, Luis R., "Informe Sobre el Rito de Purificación del Recién Nacido y de Su Madre entre los Makiritare," *Antropológica*, No. 14 (1965), 61-63. (Based on a report by Juan Francisco Nothomb.)

Wilbert, Johannes, *Indios de la Región Orinoco-Ventuari.* Caracas: 1963.

ETHNOGRAPHIC FILM

Tanzfest. ("Dance Festival.") Meinhard Schuster. 1955. 9 min. Color. Copies may be ordered from Institut für den Wissenschaftlichen Film, 34 Göttingen, Nonnenstieg 72, Germany.

5 The Pastoralists: The Goajiro of the La Guajira Peninsula

The discovery of yuca and horticulture has already been singled out as a possible contribution of Venezuelan Indians. The tremendous importance of this invention for all of tropical South America can hardly be exaggerated. Now we have to point to yet another singular achievement of Venezuelan/Colombian Indians: namely, the adoption of cattle pastoralism by the Goajiro Indians in La Guajira. The acquisition of cattle by the Goajiro as early as 1550 caused their aboriginal hunting and gathering culture to undergo radical reorganization. Their material culture, socioeconomic system, and entire value orientation were restructured into new configurations, all of which had cattle as the focal point. A completely new type of Indian culture emerged, without precedent or parallel in the entire New World: nomadic cattle pastoralism. In comparison with cattle raising, all other subsistence activities played minor roles. So successful was this change, so vigorously did the new Goajiro culture flourish, that today, with a population of some 50,000 individuals, it is the largest tribal society of Colombia and Venezuela and one of the largest in South America. In any case, the Goajiro were successful. For once, the meeting of Indians with

European colonists did not spell doom for the indigenous society and its culture.

THE HABITAT

The Goajiro, who refer to themselves in their Arawakan language as Wayú, inhabit the arid La Guajira peninsula (Wahíri), which projects into the Caribbean Sea at 12° North latitude and 73° West longitude. Politically, La Guajira belongs to Colombia except for a narrow coastal belt to the south, under Venezuelan jurisdiction. The area represents the northernmost extension of the South American continent and comprises some 5,000 square miles of land. Its southern boundary is marked by a fault extending into this region from the Sierra Nevada de Santa Marta. A second fault, running almost perpendicular to the first, divides the peninsula into Lower Guajira, a plain, and Upper Guajira, a rugged upland region with altitudes of over 650 meters.

The Goajiro have been reported in this area since early historic times (1550). They are free to roam as they wish throughout the peninsula, impeded neither by territorial boundaries of neighboring sibs nor by the national frontier. A Goajiro expects not only pasture and water for his herd but also food and assistance for himself and his family from the owners of the sib territories he traverses.

The climate of La Guajira is predominantly hot and dry. Temperatures average over 80°F. Humidity ranges from 60 to 80 per cent, but the atmosphere is stable, and most of a year's rains pour down in a few brief storms. The water runs off quickly, and winds of 30 miles per hour, together with the prevailing heat, quickly evaporate any seasonal surface moisture. The topographic and climatologic conditions turn most of the peninsula into a desert, typically characterized by xerophytic vegetation with herbaceous annuals. It is likely that the same climatic conditions prevailed in pre-Columbian times.

LANGUAGE

All Goajiro speak Goajiran, a language of Arawakan affiliation. Linguists have observed a number of different dialects within La Guajira, but the linguistic variation is never large enough to impede free communication. The five most important dialects have been regionally identified as central, arribero, abajero, playero, and serrano.

MATERIAL CULTURE AND TECHNOLOGY

Since colonial times, the Goajiro have been known for their rather special garb, that of the men being less elaborate and original than that of the women. Going about his daily chores, a man wears a short loincloth, fastened around his waist by means of a simple string or a sash adorned at its extremities with small tassels. This belt also holds a knitted string bag and a knife. A man's arrows are carried in an immense sash. In addition, he may wear a shirt or jacket. He almost always keeps his short hair tied back with a turban-like cloth or a ring of plaited straw around his head. The crown is left uncovered, and the ends of his headdress loosely dangle down his neck. Sometimes he may also put on a straw hat with a very wide brim. More often, however, it is the women who wear straw hats, fastened over their neck-long hair with a kerchief. For protection against the hot sun and blowing sand, the kerchief is allowed to hang over the face like a veil. More commonly, the women wear kerchiefs without a hat. These kerchiefs are square pieces of colorful cotton material, preferably so large that when they are folded diagonally the ends reach to the waist. Goajira women wear an ample tunic-like dress, called manta, with short sleeves. The manta reaches to their feet and gives them a most elegant

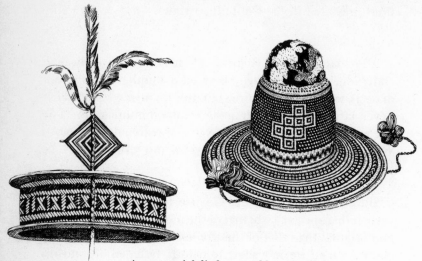

A ceremonial diadem, used by a Goajiro
man (*left*), and a man's hat (*right*).

air, especially when it is made of some rich material. Colorful flower, fruit, and animal patterns are preferred. An
expensive manta, especially one of silk, is the pride and
dream of every Goajiro woman, but one would never know
it from the nonchalant, matter-of-fact way in which she
wears it. Under their mantas women wear their pre-
puberty breechclouts fastened with beads of one or more
colors. There is an interesting difference in the attitude
of Goajiro men and women toward their native costume in
relation to the outside world: men frequently drop their
traditional attire in favor of that of their Creole neighbors,
whereas women seem to continue to feel quite comfortable
in their mantas.

To protect their feet from the hot sand, both sexes wear
sandals. These commonly consist of a leather sole with a
heel and a front strap, made either of leather or of bands

of cotton string, that passes between the big toe and the second toe. Women fasten to the front strap a big solid-color pompon, which sits right on the top of the foot, adding a fancy note to this rustic footwear.

The most typical and most valued possession of a Goajiro woman is a necklace of polished tuma stones, said to have been imported early in the colonial period by European traders. Tumas are of a pale reddish color, almost pink, some 5 millimeters in diameter and strung on a twisted cotton string. Interspersed with tumas may be archaeological gold beads (found in Tairona graves). The center of the necklace may be accentuated by an irregular group of tumas, and the end of the chain decorated with golden miniature representations of turtles, frogs, or other animals. A necklace of this kind is priceless; it passes from a mother to her eldest daughter and remains in the possession of the sib or casta. If a woman dies without female offspring, the necklace passes on to her next youngest sister. A woman's bride-price is determined to a considerable degree by the tuma necklaces and other necklaces of high value in her possession. Necklaces of lesser worth are made of cornalina stones and corals. Bracelets, anklets, rings, and earrings are also worn by the women.

Body paint is of great cosmetic importance to a Goajiro woman. Yellow, brown, and black powders, produced by pulverizing the crusty bark of certain trees, are kept in elongated calabashes and applied to face, neck, and arms with a cloth puff. In preparation, the body parts to be decorated are covered with a fine layer of sheep's tallow. Among the trees that have been mentioned as producing the desired powders are aceituno, cují, guásimo, kaisto, and others. The kaisto wood itself is reduced to charcoal and pulverized to produce an intensely black stain for body painting. A red substance applied to lips, cheeks, and forehead is prepared by boiling down the leaves of the palisa tree. The residual paste is left to cool overnight, then pulverized, and mixed with oil before use. While reducing the leaves to a pomade, a woman abstains from food and drink to ensure successful completion of the process. The powder of a mushroom is also used as a paint. Finally, there are at least two kinds of plant juice employed for the same purpose. One is prepared by pressing the fruit of the guanapay tree until the interior of the fruit is reduced to a juicy pulp. The juice is applied to cheeks, forehead, nose, neck, and arms by means of a pointed stick repeatedly pushed into the fruit. The guanapay juice is used to paint geometrical designs on the skin. Curiously, at the moment of application the paint is invisible, but it soon changes to an intensive blue. The sap of the kasis bush is also collected as a body paint. It is usually applied with a stick to make spots of various sizes on the face. These spots can be left "natural"—that is, a pale blue—or covered with one of the powders of pulverized bark. Plant juices are used mainly as a means of beautification. The different paints and pastes produced from barks, mushrooms, kaisto wood, and boiled-down palisa leaves, in combination with tallow, serve the added function of protecting the woman's exposed body parts from the effects of intense sunshine. All body paints are easily removed by simple washing.

Goajiro women know how to spin and weave. Wild cotton is used often; the wool of sheep, rarely. Yarns may be left natural or colored with vegetable dyes. The loom consists of two thick horizontal poles. One is attached firmly under the roof beam or between two uprights; the other either hangs loose from the warp thread or is fastened to a pole in the ground some distance away from the house or from the uprights. A continuous thread is wound around the two horizontal poles. The woman, seated in front of the loom, passes the shuttle by hand; the warp is shifted with the help of a device that takes hold of alternate strands. The finished cloth is wound around the poles in an endless strip, which is cut into the desired lengths. The Goajiro are famous for their durable and exquisitely woven hammocks and also for other textile products, such as bright-colored belts for the men and their horses, sashes, and bags. Large mats of a reed called enea, a perennial marsh plant, are also woven by the women, for use variously as internal walls for houses, sleeping mats, etc.

Only a few local groups, living in the vicinity of the Teta, a mountain near the center of the peninsula, make crude pottery. Sometimes clay is exported from there to other parts of La Guajira, to be made into the essential earthenware containers. The Goajiro produce mainly cooking pots, large water jugs, and wide urns with narrow necks for secondary burial. The woman potter kneads the clay thoroughly by means of a stone or bottle, while adding water in which ground divi-divi was left to soak for a day. The clay thus prepared is rolled into long coils, some 1.5 centimeters thick, which are used to build the pot. The beginning of the coil is placed on a prefabricated concave plate, which serves as a form for the round bottom of the

A Goajiro pot and a pottery water jug in a woven carrying net.

container. Newly made pieces are left to dry in the sun for three days before firing. At this time, the pots are decorated with whatever designs are desired. For this purpose, a special reddish clay from the Upper Guajira is diluted with water and applied with the fingers. The dried vessels are then placed together in a hole excavated in the sand and a fire of donkey dung is kept going around them for about one hour. After cooling, the new ware is ready for use.

Goajiro houses are not very elaborate; a migrating group will often be satisfied with a mere windscreen, an arbor, or a temporary gabled roof supported on poles—a reminder of bygone days, when the Goajiro were nomadic hunter-gatherers. More frequently, however, a family will also construct a more permanent house with a gabled roof and exterior walls of wattle-and-daub. Thatch is prepared from sara palm leaves, enea, or cactus split lengthwise. Brick and cement houses with metal roofs are also becoming more frequent. Horizontal living space inside these more elaborate houses is quite limited. The frame structure of the walls is from 3 to 4 meters in height, windows are small quadrangular openings, and doors are narrow. Protective cactus hedges are drawn around more permanent villages. Local groups live in extended rancherías, with up to 50 houses and 100 to 250 inhabitants. Houses are built at gunshot distance from each other to avoid surprise attacks.

The Goajiro today obtain most of the tools they use from the Creoles through extensive trade. These include mainly machetes, axes, knives, metal containers, and firearms. Rifles and ammunition are quite expensive and preserved for warfare rather than used on the hunt. For this reason, bows and arrows are still the principal hunting weapons.

Bows are made of the elastic wood of the manaca palm.

In cross-section the 2-meter-long bow is almost round. The string is made of sisal cordage. The Goajiro bowman protects his wrist from the backsnapping string by means of a decorated leather strap. Arrows are some 1.5 meters long, with different kinds of points. Rather common is a point made of manaca wood, 20 centimeters long and round, triangular, or quadrangular in cross-section. Carved along the edges of these manaca points are rows of notches pointed toward the shaft, which prevent the arrow from slipping out of the wounded animal. Arrow points are also made of sting-ray spines, scrap iron, nails, cartridge cases, and large, rounded, wooden knobs about 2.5 centimeters in diameter. The latter are used to stun birds; nail-tipped arrows are used for small game; and metal-tipped arrows serve in warfare. Metal points are fastened to a 15-20-centimeter-long foreshaft of hard wood, the other end of which is inserted in the shaft of arrowreed.

Goajira arrows are feathered, and their tips are frequently saturated in a poison made of mashed scorpions, centipedes, poisonous spiders, and snake venom. The mixture, which retains its potency for about six months, is kept in a short bamboo container, which the hunter or warrior carries fastened to his waist close to the arrow points in their individual hollow-reed containers. Before shooting, the points are dipped into the venom, which is much feared among the Goajiro themselves as well as by their extratribal enemies.

The Goajiro make only a few musical instruments. Dances are rhythmically accompanied by swinging a calabash rattle filled with stones. A percussion instrument is the tambour drum, about a half-meter high and 30 centimeters in diameter, made of wood of parcha, ceiba, or jabillo. The drumheads at either end are covered with the skin of a sheep, kept tight by means of cocuiza rope and small wooden toggles. The Goajiro drum is played with one or two drumsticks. The drummer will play it with the instrument hanging from the rafter of the house, from his neck, standing before him on the ground, or held between his knees. Two wind instruments, a clarinet and a fife, have also been observed among the Goajiro. The former is made of a 60-centimeter-long reed, with a vibrating reed in the mouthpiece and a calabash at the other end of a resonance chamber. This instrument is side-blown. Reed or bamboo fifes are rare. More common is the jew's harp (terempe) made of metal and ornamented with colored tassels. Men and even small boys play these instruments with great skill and carry them fastened to their belts.

FOOD-QUEST ACTIVITIES

Most of the pre-Columbian Goajiro probably subsisted by hunting and gathering in the interior, and by collecting shellfish on the coast, although maritime exploitation is seriously restricted by the scarcity of fresh water in the coastal areas.

The collecting of wild vegetable foods is still practiced to some extent by Goajira women and girls, especially during periods of scarcity or famine. The roots of enea are edible—atlhough only after a somewhat laborious process of preparation, in the course of which the roots are peeled, diced, sun-dried, grated, leeched, and boiled in water for about three hours over a slow fire. The resulting porridge has to be eaten on the same day it was prepared lest it become acid and unpalatable. However, the dried roots, either in diced form or as flour, can be stored for a longer period of time without spoiling. The fruit of the divi-divi tree and the fruits of such cacti as cardón, breva, tuna, and buche are also eaten. Of the cardón cactus the Goajiro also eat the peeled and fried heart. In pre-agricultural times this gathering activity must have been quite important to Goajiro existence; nowadays both the taste for such wild foods and the know-how of their preparation have been largely lost. Nevertheless, there remains a long list of edible wild foods of considerable importance as a backstop for hard times.

Early chroniclers reported that the Goajiro relied mainly on hunting for the procurement of their food. Today, however, hunting occupies a minor place in the Goajiro economy. Deer, rabbits, peccary, and birds constitute the chief game. Rifles or, more frequently, bow and arrow are used as weapons, and hunting traps, made of wood and grass fibers, have also been reported. Fishing, when practiced at all, is of importance only along the lagoons and coasts. Nets and hook and line are the principal methods employed. Lobster, mollusks, and crabs are also caught.

Farming is very poorly developed and is practiced in only a few areas, around the foothills. Plants cultivated include plantains, maguey, onions, coca, sugar cane, bananas, corn, gourds, manioc, sweet potatoes, millet, beans, and watermelons. Some tobacco is also grown. Cattle-raising Goajiro may also clear the brush around their semipermanent camps to plant small patches of fast-maturing corn shortly before the rainy season. The women harvest after the rains have stopped and use the kernels to brew chicha beer.

Soon after contact, the Goajiro underwent an economic revolution. Controlling rich pearl beds, these Indians began to trade with the Europeans and soon acquired sheep, goats, pigs, chickens, and—most important—horses, donkeys, and cattle. The Goajiro adopted nomadic goat-herding, probably from the expert Spaniards, and nomadic cattle-herding *possibly* from the Europeans and their own newly acquired Negro slaves. By 1550, cattle were already quite abundant in the peninsula. A completely new type of Indian culture emerged, without precedent or parallel in the entire New World: cattle pastoralism. In comparison with cattle raising, other subsistence activities assumed minor importance, and meat and milk products became the basic diet of the Goajiro. Cattle not only were economically integrated but, as will be shown later on, also became the ultimate measure of the social system and the value system. The meat of their domestic animals as well as several byproducts, such as skin, are Goajiro trade goods which fetch a good price on nearby Creole markets. With the money they receive, the Indians can buy all the foods and merchandise they do not themselves produce, which they have learned to appreciate. Cattle pastoralism forces a seminomadic pattern on the tribe, who roam about La Guajira with their herds in search of fodder and water.

The men and boys of the family perform the many tasks associated with tending the herds and caring for the livestock in general. The women and girls process all vegetables, as well as meat, milk, and cheese. The most common drink is water, but the women also make a gruel with a base of corn and crude sugar. The corn is either masticated by the women before the brewing process begins or simply pulverized on a flat stone. Corn beer is drunk in considerable quantities. Rum is received through trade, and festivals tend to become quite lively as a result of the rather generous consumption of this intoxicant. Women roll long, thin cigars of eight to ten leaves of tobacco. Goajiro in the western part of the peninsula also used to grow and chew coca, a practice possibly learned from their Chibchan neighbors.

SOCIAL ORGANIZATION

The social organization of the Goajiro is characterized by extended families with polygynous households. The most important dividing line in intra- or extra-group relations is the distinction the Goajiro make between "blood-

relatives" (agnatic or patrilineal) and "flesh-relatives" (uterine or matrilineal). Kinship ties among "flesh-relatives," referred to as "casta," are considered to be stronger than
those between patrilineal relatives.* Frequently we find
the extended family clustered around the homestead of the
maternal uncle. Otherwise, residence is matrilocal and the
groom lives with the family of his wife. Polygyny is a mark
of status and rank. It is quite permissible for a man to
marry two women who are consanguineal sisters, although
this practice occurs rarely.

These customs correspond to a kinship system of the
Crow type, and the tribe is subdivided into some thirty
sibs or "castas," each in possession of its own territory and
identified with an animal. There is no central government,
but each sib respects the senior mother's brother, who represents the highest authority within the uterine descent
group. His office of "chief" is matrilineally inherited.
Hereditary status is very important and is based largely
on the accumulated wealth of the individual, his family,
and his sib.

The maternal uncle is an adviser and, above all, a legal
representative. It may happen, for instance, that an adolescent kills someone else's cow. To claim compensation, the
offended party will go, not to the boy's father, but to his
maternal uncle. After the claim has been made, the uncle
will reproach the boy's mother and demand her help in
providing the stipulated compensation. But should she not
be in a position to comply, the maternal uncle will be left

* We employ the Spanish term *casta* as used in La Guajira to designate
the extended family, lineage, and sib. Today, casta members tend to dis-
regard the customary rule of exogamous marriage as soon as the actual
matrilineal relationship can no longer be traced. The Goajiro recognize
some forty castas, but while both sexes inherit their mother's flesh, it is
only through the females of each generation that flesh can be passed on
to the next. (Data on social organization and the life cycle have been published in a different form and greater detail in Wilbert, 1970.)

with the full debt. There are other cases where the nephew commits a serious offense for which the offended lineage requests the life of the boy as compensation. The uncle will not permit the murder of his nephew and will oppose the offended party against the customary law in favor of the interests of the lineage. No distinction according to sex or age is made so long as the life taken in compensation is part of the offender's casta. The *lex talionis* of Goajiro customary law must be satisfied.

In most cases it seems that the uncle's offer to die for his nephew represents only a daring challenge. However, if accepted, it becomes a declaration of war and starts one of the many seemingly perpetual feuds among so-called enemies of the flesh. Such feuds may go on for many generations, and everyone born to the offender's lineage is as guilty of the original crime as was his avuncular ancestor. Time rarely heals the wounds. Every morning the mother of the murdered person or another kinsman recites the atrocious deed that caused the death of her son or kinsman and any subsequent calamity brought about by the feud. This morning recital goes on for generations, keeping the crime vivid in the minds of the offended lineage's kinfolk.

The maternal uncle's legal responsibility for his sister's children is all-inclusive. The nephew will take his uncle's place after the latter has passed away. To mark his position, the sister's son is referred to as awúliaajuna, "the shoot that sprouts at the base of the stem."

To the same extent that the maternal uncle is liable for his nephew's misdeeds, so the inheritance is passed on from the older to the younger. After the uncle has died, the nephew, who will succeed him in a political leadership role of a wealthy lineage, will fully realize that all the benefits he has received from his uncle were actually entrusted to him. Now it is he who has to administer the wealth of the lineage and protect the interests of lineage and sib, with his own life if necessary. He is not able himself to perpetuate his flesh, but he must create the optimal conditions for the welfare and perpetuation of the casta through his uterine kinswomen. Wealth creates these favorable circumstances, and his wealth must remain closely linked with the lineage.

Girls also turn to their maternal uncle as their main helper and adviser, though in matters specifically feminine a maternal aunt or a maternal grandmother are more naturally consulted.

Like the child's mother, although to a lesser extent, the maternal uncle establishes a personal "savings account" for the child as a birthday present. Usually the gift consists of animals—goats, cattle, or horses—which the child cannot dispose of. Instead, these animals, together with others the child may receive as gifts from friends and relatives, are entrusted to the care of a herdsman, who receives as compensation the byproduct of the growing herd, plus one female animal per year.

Besides the two loci of authority—the mother (and in a limited way also the father) within the nuclear family and the maternal uncle within the lineage segment—there emerges from time to time a chief who wields paramount power over the entire lineage. He becomes known as the judge of the casta. He is able to resolve disputes between members of the lineage and represents the maximum authority to pass judgment in cases that concern the lineage —for example, those involving homicide or blood revenge.

The Goajiro are the only Venezuelan Indian society organized unilineally in sibs. The unilineal descent group is almost a sacrosanct institution to these Indians and is one of the main reasons the Goajiro have survived as a vigorous tribe. The individual's life is eternally protected within his casta, and he will do anything to defend his sib in times of crisis. The casta is a socially and economically integrated system perpetuated through the women and the cattle. The value of the casta, its women and men, stands in direct proportion to the value of the cattle it possesses.

It is quite extraordinary to see how strongly, in an American Indian society, the casta in general and the individual woman in particular are identified with cattle. Murder, the violent annihilation of a part of the casta, can be compensated with an appropriately large number of cattle. Theft of cattle and other livestock is punished as severely as sexual violation of a woman. The payment is very high in both cases and is made to satisfy the abused honor of the casta. The identity of cattle with human beings (flesh) also is obvious in the practice of having sick cattle, like sick humans, treated by shamans. On his wedding night, the groom gives his mother-in-law several head of cattle as payment for the nuptial hammock and the right to sleep with the bride. The bride-price is expressed in a quantity of cattle and equine livestock. Since cattle legitimize the rebirth of the flesh through matrimony, they become of key importance for the continuation of the casta. In the cattle lies the fate of the lineage to prosper or decline. Years ago, it was reported, women who were not paid for in cattle were expelled from their lineage, and their children were denied social recognition as the flesh of their matri-kinsmen. A Goajiro woman expressed this identity between livestock and man in the following way: "I was very pleased when I had a boy child. I considered him to be a little horse, and I regarded my little daughter as if she were a little cow, since cows are the greatest wealth we possess." Cattle sacrificed during a wake must not be consumed by the relatives of the deceased, because this would be equal to eating the flesh of the dead. And, finally, a woman eating of her cattle commits incest—that is, mixes the flesh. There is a causal connection between the casta and its cattle: one cannot exist without the other.

The preservation and regeneration of the casta and the defense of its wealth are responsibilities that rest heavily on Goajiro men and women of reproductive age. The mother fosters in her offspring and other lineage-folk an understanding of their historic origin. Within the lineage, the genealogical ancestry and ties connecting individuals to one another are recognized to a depth of some three generations. A man's and a woman's allegiance to these representatives of the lineage is unconditional. The members of a maximal matrilineage recognize their relationship even if their matrilineal descent line cannot be traced back genealogically in every case. The living lineage members assume collective responsibility for their ancestors and for each other.

The lineage has the recognized right to request compensation for any loss of blood that occurs, whether this be a consequence of voluntary or involuntary action, and whether it be through self-injury or through the intervention of a second person. The price that the lineage will request in compensation for any loss of their blood depends on the actual socioeconomic value of the group and the striking power of its men. A man pays for the blood his wife loses in defloration and childbirth, and also for miscarriages. Cobro (payment) is requested in compensation for a wound that one child in playing inflicts on another from a different lineage. To avoid cobro, women will forcibly remove their intoxicated men from rowdy crowds. Even pain requires cobro. For instance, after an unsuccessful attempt at suicide, the clan will claim damages from the one who drove the person to attempt suicide, even if no blood has been shed. The maternal uncle enforces the customary law according to the wealth and power of his matri-kinsmen. He files his cobro claim according to the status of his own casta; he pays indemnities commensurate with the rank of the casta offended. In particular cases,

even paternal kinsmen demand "tear money" in compensation for inflicted grief. Another set of cobro regulations
protects the female of the casta from abuse of her reproductive power.

If cobro demands are not satisfied, the offended casta
will attempt to remove forcibly what they consider to be
rightfully theirs. In such cases the women of the casta will
bring forth the magical war contras, charms which they
have inherited from the preceding generation. They have
guarded these charms as an ultimate resource for protection;
they have received visions from the contras, and they will
transfer their power to the men who set out to engage the
enemy. Sons of fighting age are expected to side with their
mother's casta against that of their father if these two are
at odds, and a husband with his own casta against that of
his wife and children.

LIFE CYCLE AND RELIGIOUS BELIEFS

It has been said that Goajiro women use contraceptives
to space their children. A woman who longs for her first
child or whose youngest child has reached age at which
independent living is deemed possible discontinues contra-
ceptive measures and prepares herself for pregnancy. The
Goajiro believe that fertilization takes place when the
semen of the man mixes with the woman's menstrual blood
in the uterus.

The Goajiro mother conceives her new baby as a homunculus, a tiny old man, which floats about in the fetal fluid
for a period of nine months, nourished by the menstrual
blood of the mother. That is why menstruation stops with
conception. Because of this initial condition at the time of
conception, the growing child in the womb has three basic
components: the flesh of the mother, comparable to the
yolk of the egg; the initially small portion of uterine blood,
comparable to the red dot within the yolk; and the "blood"

1   Goajiro houses are often only temporary structures
with gabled roofs of split cactus and reed-mat walls.

During the
dry season,
water must be
fetched from
wells or casimbas,
frequently more
than 10 meters
deep.

Watering the cattle.

A Goajiro woman
spinning wild cotton,
turning the end of
the spindle in a
calabash.

4

As transportation animals, mules are valued more than horses in La Guajira.

A migrating Goajiro mother and her children take the mat from their house along to the new locality.

Goajiro women and children.

The brisk steps of the chichamaya dance.

of the father, comparable to the egg white. Like the red matter in the egg, the quantity of uterine blood is quite small within the homunculus; but it will increase and progressively displace the agnatic blood until, at the end of life, the agnatic blood has almost disappeared, having given way to the uterine blood generated by the flesh.

The expectant mother will go out at night into the desert to talk to the newcomer in her womb. She asks him who he is, whether he comes from an ancient, a more recent, or her present generation. The mother knows that she may be giving flesh and form to a matrilineal ancestor who will be reincarnated in the same flesh that has been passed on to her through a long chain of uterine relatives, stemming ultimately from the original ancestress of a remote past.

For this reason, birth or rebirth is the exclusive responsibility of the matrilineage; the expected new life partakes of all its members. The father is less importantly involved, although at the time of birth and during early infancy child and father are more closely related to each other than at any time thereafter.

The matrilineal kinsmen watch over their pregnant relative to make sure that taboos and prescriptions are rigorously observed. The pregnant woman and her husband must strictly avoid everything connected with burial and disinterment ceremonies. Witnessing death rituals retards the birth of the new kinsman, especially if the woman is present during the lowering of the corpse into the grave. The woman's female kinsmen normally also assume the responsibility of preparing and administering medicines during labor. They stand by during delivery, massage the womb of the woman, and physically support her.

This is why a woman goes to her mother or other matrilineal female kinsmen to be delivered of her child. Among most of the Goajiro only the matrilineal relatives are allowed to be present during labor and childbirth. Should ill fortune befall the mother, and should she die in childbirth, the maternal kin are held responsible, and the bride-price has to be restored to the widower. (This is not the case if delivery takes place away from the mother's maternal kinsmen's home.) The child is left with its maternal grandmother or maternal aunt, and the father returns to his maternal kinfolk.

A stillborn child is not buried in the lineage cemetery. Instead, it is placed head down in an urn and buried under a special tree, called hururá, in a grave dug by his oldest maternal uncle. The parents are prevented from attending the burial lest their future children suffer the same ill fortune. The situation disallows profound grief on the part of the parents. The mother of the stillborn child must submit to a second, though shorter, version of the blanqueo or puberty confinement to undo any possible errors and transgressions of taboos that occurred during her first confinement.

It is obvious that within such a conceptual framework abortion must be considered a crime and an act of aggression against the entire casta. After careful examination, the party deemed to have provoked such an incident will be held responsible.

The newly reborn kinsman's period of reinstatement into the world of the living begins the minute he leaves his mother's womb. His identification with, and his position within, the matrilineal descent group and sib are automatic. He is received and accepted by the various members of his matrilineage who witness his passage into the world, and the female relatives of the child take an interest in his well-being. In contrast to the strong interest displayed by the casta kinfolk of the newborn, the father's behavior is much more reserved; agnatic relatives of the infant may even choose to ignore him at this time. Nevertheless, gifts may be given to the child by his father and other relatives. Gift-giving by relatives and friends depends to a large extent on whether the mother of the child "turned out well." If she is a woman of exemplary behavior, who married well and caused her parents no embarrassment (for instance, because she wasn't a virgin), her children, as when they are born, will receive numerous gifts from both paternal and maternal relatives. If the mother has turned out badly, on the other hand, her children will receive few or no gifts from their relatives. In other words, the mother's legitimate marriage and her exercise of valid reproductive powers are rewarded by kinsmen who strengthen the chances of the survival of their own lineage through gift-giving. Generally, uterine relatives are cautious about giving away livestock, the economic guarantee of the lineage. A mother who "turned out well" does not always produce good children. The maternal grandmother and even the child's own mother prefer to give their gifts of animals only after the child has grown up a little and has demonstrated to their satisfaction that he is able to care for them himself.

The identification of the newborn is of great importance to his uterine kinsmen, who soon discuss the name for the child. The mother seems to have the traditional right to name her children after her ancestors or living maternal kinsmen. As in other societies, such a personal name is more or less secret, is used only by his close relatives and friends, and remains an individual's most intimate possession throughout life and after death. Whoever mentions a person's name outside his closest circle is guilty of a grave offense and is held liable for it. (The consequences of mentioning the name of a dead person will be described later.)

In addition to his personal name, the child inherits his sib name also, which is used in the manner of a surname.

Generally, however, the child is known by a nickname, which his parents or relatives bestow upon him according to a distinguishing body mark or some occurrence during his birth. Nowadays, Christian names are also frequently used. After the birth of their first child, the parents become known by a teknonym (the prefix "mother of so-and-so" or "father of so-and-so" followed by the name of the child).

The bond between mother and child is the strongest and most transcendent in Goajiro society. During the first one and a half to two years, the child is the focus of attention. At the time of weaning, however, this attitude changes abruptly, and motherly affection and warmth are replaced by efficiency and formality. His mother will now guide him toward the next major episode of his life. Strict regulations govern this process of growth, and any deviation from the norm is severely punished. The child has to obey without fault. Gradually he will have to adjust to his new status, look after himself, and assume social responsibilities on his own. In the course of a rather violent socialization process, coolness comes to replace warmth and respect replaces love, sometimes creating feelings of frustration through childhood and adolescence which appear to fall little short of hatred. Nevertheless, the close bond of unique specificity between mother and child is recognized and defended through life. The adult offspring becomes more and more aware of the role that the mother plays in accepting responsibility for the preservation of the lineage.

Generally the Goajiro father assumes an increasingly reserved attitude toward his children as they grow older. He may play with them as youngsters, and may offer help and advice later, but his role in their socialization after they reach adolescence is negligible. A reason for this detached attitude may lie in the fact that a Goajiro father lacks any legal authority over his children and has no continuing legal obligations toward them. The gifts of animals and other property he bestows on his young children are voluntary tokens of his love and affection, not an inheritance.

Goajiro children grow up loving their grandparents, who take reciprocal pleasure and pride in their grandchildren. Of special importance and closeness is the maternal grandmother, who frequently helps deliver the child, often takes care of him in the mother's absence, plays with him, gives him his bath, and shields him from his mother's anger. As an adolescent the Goajira youngster seeks his grandparents' advice. The girls especially confide heavily in the grandmother, who is the origin of all casta members around them.

The behavior of a child or adolescent toward his parents is respectful and reserved. From early childhood, however, a more intimate rapport is fostered between nephews and their maternal uncles. The uncle may come to visit his nephew, to encourage him, teach him, and in general help him grow up. He will lift him for the first time into a saddle, and he will show him the work around the herds. The nephew will learn that many of the cattle and the horses belonging to his uncle are equally his own property, and that the uncle is teaching him how to take care of them. The nephew is allowed to ride even the horse reserved for the uncle's exclusive use. In well-to-do families, the maternal uncle will take special care to teach his ten-year-old nephew how to compete in the Goajiro's favorite sport of horse racing. The first shotgun the boy owns is a present from his maternal uncle.

Within the sibling group, differences in age and sex carry important social distinctions. The eldest son occupies the ranking position within the sibling class. In domestic affairs he is consulted by his mother even when he is still very small. In the absence of his father he assumes the latter's decision-making functions, which are observed by his younger siblings as if they had been exercised by their father. The older boy also enjoys the right to the choicest helpings of food, as well as the attentions of his mother and sisters in respect to his own personal comfort.

In general, the older sibling has definite authority over the younger ones, and siblings are expected to maintain respectful and harmonious relationships among themselves. Avoidance taboos are not observed among siblings, but from an early age the children of the two sexes are socialized in strongly segregated fashion according to stereotype norms for specific male and female roles. Siblings are taught to assume a mutually supportive attitude toward each other. Rudeness and aggressiveness between adolescent brothers and sisters are quite common but are overcome in later years. Any hostile feelings are then replaced by restrained amicability among the young adults, who firmly rely on one another's support through life.

Within the nuclear family, a brother's legal power over his sister becomes apparent very early in the boy's life. The power is vested in him because he is the nearest male relative of the same casta. This condition is recognized by his sister and by the boy's mother, who yields to his authority. The brother's attitude toward his sister, in turn, is conditioned by the same consideration that conditions a maternal uncle's attitude toward his niece: it is through these female relatives that their casta will be perpetuated.

The Goajiro consider their children to be miniature adults from the time they are two years old. Chief responsibility for their proper socialization rests with their mother. But the responsibility for the children's socialization is shared by both parents and by the adults of the entire matrilineage.

A Goajiro boy at the age of three accompanies his father and brothers to the well, the herd, and the field, where he can start learning about a man's occupation by watching the men. By the age of five he has learned the fundamentals of herding and starts taking care of a small flock of sheep and goats by himself. Between eight and twelve years of age the boy is able to take care of a larger herd of cattle, horses, burros, and mules. Observation and imitation are supplemented by instructions given the boy by his father or his maternal uncle. From about the ninth year, the uncle intervenes more and more in the boy's instruction, and frequently the boy goes to live with his maternal uncle for long periods of time. Here the boy takes care of the uncle's herds, which may become his own later on in his life. The uncle may also take him on hunting expeditions. He will acquire the skills of manufacturing and manipulating weapons—the same weapons he will use on war parties in defense of his lineage. A boy of thirteen or fourteen is considered old enough to take an active part in warfare. Through his continued contact in common residence, the maternal uncle has ample opportunity to test his nephew's mettle. The nephew, challenged by his apprenticeship, feels strongly motivated to meet his uncle's expectations, so as to be rewarded with a rich inheritance. While the mother continues to play an important role in her son's upbringing throughout this period, the maternal uncle will take an increasing part in the boy's education. The male adults of the matrilineage are quite conscious of the fact that the prosperous perpetuation of their lineage depends on the skills and defensive strength of their nephews, and such training cannot be left in the hands of their kinswomen.

The mother teaches her young girls all the domestic chores that are typically the work of Goajiro women. Just as young boys are criticized when they stay around their mother too much, the girls are taught that cattle raising is exclusively the man's domain. At three a girl starts tending the fire and the house. At six she begins to cook and take care of her younger siblings; at ten or eleven she is familiar with most of the economic functions of an adult woman.

The Goajiro girl must acquire the important skills of weaving, needlework, and embroidery. Shortly before puberty, when she starts learning these arts, the girl leaves her mother's house for a period of months, or even years, to move into the household of a maternal aunt known for her artistry. This co-residence of the niece with her maternal aunt (a classificatory "mother") also provides a gentle changeover from instruction in economic duties to the teaching of matters related to sex and reproduction.

The family and the matrilineage are the omnipresent forces that shape the Goajiro child and adolescent. The casta establishes itself early in the minds of these young people as the pivot on which life turns. Through indoctrination during childhood and adolescence, the casta assures its economic stability, continued protection, and physical perpetuation. Play as a pastime is unproductive in this sense. For children to play with children of other lineages is even dangerous, inasmuch as bloodshed (hence legal dispute) may result. Pain and sickness are the first signs of possible decline, and the mother and her matri-kin are much concerned with the health of the young. Since the upbringing of the children is so vital a matter for the entire matrilineage, maternal aunts, uncles, and grandmothers are interchangeable with the mother as educators. Before the child actually enters the world of adults he has become quite aware of his personal responsibility for his casta and has learned to cherish solidarity as the buttress of the matrilineage. Sibling disharmony, dishonesty, premarital heterosexual relations, homosexuality, wastefulness, laziness, lack of altruism toward matri-kinsmen, recklessness, sickness, and so forth are alarming threats to the matrilineage, to be avoided and eradicated at all costs. The child constantly feels and breathes the demanding basic rules of the matrilineage, both living and dead.

At puberty the matrilineal kinswomen make a special effort to prepare the girl; they assume full responsibility for any failures in this respect. They do all in their power to have her leave the puberty seclusion as desirable to the men and as valuable to the casta as possible. Bolinder (1957) reports a Goajiro standard of beauty:

> How must a girl look to find favor with them [men]? She must be tall, broad-hipped and have firm, prominent breasts and well-rounded curves. Flabbiness the men do not like, but they do not seem to worry about the shape of their women's legs. . . . The Goajiro girl should have large eyes and good teeth, but the most important thing of all is that she should be light-skinned; that is the hall-mark of gentility. . . . The rules she has to observe and the medicines she must take are of importance not only for her appearance, but also for her physique. If she follows her instructions, she will give birth without difficulty and there will be no risk of the baby being stillborn.

On the day of her first menstruation, the girl is washed with cold water to ensure light skin, and she is given an herbal drink to induce vomiting. This ritual cleansing causes the expulsion from the body of all elements that pertain to childhood. The hair (of childhood) is cut, placed in a bag, and hidden. Next the girl is dressed in the wide manta of a Goajiro woman. Aphrodisiac love charms or contras are placed on her body, especially on her breasts and genitals. Finally, the girl is laid in a hammock and hoisted to the top of the roof, or else she is confined within the house to a special compartment set up for this purpose. The girl is not allowed to eat solid foods. Only liquids are allowed, and those are taken to induce more vomiting. During the seclusion of several days, the girl has to remain motionless. Furthermore, she must not scratch herself or step or spit on the floor, because these actions would make her less desirable to the man she hopes to marry.

While the girl is undergoing this ordeal her parents invite relatives and friends to a festival in order to mark the occasion. The dance of the chicha maya, a fertility dance, is central to the festivities, which last several days. At the end of the fiesta the initiate is taken to a special hut, or a secluded part of the house, to begin the isolation stage, the so-called blanqueo.

The blanqueo may last for months and even years, depending on the social status and affluence of the girl's family. During this time the girl has to avoid the sun and may leave her hut only at night. The men must not see her during this period of formation. From a grass of the Harara Mountains the lineage women prepare a drink which, taken twice daily by the girl, is believed to give her body the fore-mentioned ideal features and prevent her from growing old prematurely. It is most important for her future well-being, however, that she also take the necessary potions which prevent her from menstruating during the confinement. Still other potions guarantee her future fertility.

The blanqueo is also a period of instruction. The young girl learns about her socioeconomic role as an adult woman, as well as about matters concerning sexual and reproductive preparedness. She is taught the significance of the various charms and contras and how these may be used to ensure attractiveness and a high bride-price in marriage, which are values of great importance to her. She is also taught the ritual taboos and prohibitions connected with marriage, pregnancy, and birth, as well as the supernatural rationale that underlies them.

Toward the end of the blanqueo, the duration of which is determined by the maternal relatives, the girl gradually leaves her puberty confinement. First she ventures into the hallway, then into the entire house, and finally into the open air. The girl emerging from the darkness of the blanqueo is bathed with pitchers of cold water. Her hair is cut, and she is clothed in a woman's brightly colored dress. Ornaments are put on her, and her face is decorated with the red onoto designs of an adult woman.

The termination of the blanqueo is marked by official reinstatement—a "coming out" festival of several days, which is attended by eligible bachelors. The girl is formally presented at midnight, and she is bathed by several female kinsmen behind a screen while her guests dance. Next, while she is still within her family of orientation, follows a period of practicing the woman's skills she acquired during the blanqueo. This final period of apprenticeship in most cases does not last long. Suitors visit the girl under supervision, on the pretext of ordering woven articles from her. If the girl aspires to marry one man in particular, she rubs her body with the aphrodisiac charms and avoids roasted food, milk, and the fire. She has buried clippings of the first post-blanqueo growth of her hair under cow dung to attract this or that wealthy man, capable of paying a substantial bride-price in cattle. Especially in upper-class families, virginity is highly esteemed, since its loss lowers the value of the young woman considerably.

Falling in love with and marrying one of her suitors will finally wean the young woman from her family of orientation and project her as an independent woman ready to start her own family.

The eligibility of a person as a spouse depends largely on two determining restrictions: the extension of the incest taboo, and the socioeconomic status of the prospective partners. Goajiro incest prohibitions follow one fundamental rule: lineage flesh must not mix with lineage flesh. The final decision on whether or not two would-be partners share the same flesh rests with the maternal uncle and the kinswomen of the matrilineage. Lineage exogamy is

enjoined as long as actual bonds of flesh can be traced.
Marriage between a woman and any matrilineal kinsman
is frowned upon. Marriage between a woman and her
father is also taboo. With the exception of the children of
a maternal aunt, all other first cousins are potential
spouses.

Men who commit incest become bald. Deformations in
children as a result of incest are also greatly feared. Pregnancies resulting from incestuous relations are known to
end in suicide: the expectant mother may hang herself.
Expulsion of the man at fault seems to be the rule. Incest
is a crime that by no means concerns only the couple involved in the offense. On the contrary, it is a serious matter
that concerns the entire lineage, whose intrinsic value was
undermined by the crime. The lineage's members are ridiculed as kin of beasts.

The second restrictive custom regulating marriage among
the Goajiro is class consciousness: a girl marries a boy from
a lineage economically compatible with her own. Social
status (closely linked to affluence) is important. Even if a
lower-class person could find a way to raise the high bride-
price for a rich family's girl, it would still remain question-
able whether the matrilineage of the desired bride could
overlook the difference in social status.

The official marriage ceremony is mainly a transaction
of goods and guarantees between the two lineages, which,
through this act, become keraí, in-laws, with all the obligations this relationship implies (described below in greater
detail). During the celebration the bride's kinsmen exert
themselves to receive and entertain the groom's brothers,
as well as his other kinsmen. Members of both lineages are
well aware that the bonds of marriage being established
between two of their kin represent a contract of cooperation not only for the couple but for all of them.

On a prearranged day, the two lineages meet in the house of the bride to deliver and receive the payment. Acceptance of the full price seals the bond of marriage. The bride-price should ideally be as much or more than has been paid by the bride's father and kin for her mother. To receive more in payment for the daughter has been the main objective of the negotiations carried on between the representatives of the two lineages. A groom will pride himself on his ability to provide the bride-payments himself, if he is so fortunate. Otherwise, he will have to work for many years to come in order to pay back his friends and relatives who contributed to the payment. Marriage primarily provides the husband with the right of exclusive sexual access to his wife. He can be sure that the woman will do all in her power to enhance her desirability and maintain and increase his satisfaction. Her kinsmen take a lasting interest in their kinswoman's sexual behavior, in order to assure its legitimacy and efficacy. Should the wife desert her husband, commit adultery, or fail to perform her duties as a wife and mother to the fullest expectation of the husband, the man will leave her and will demand that the bride-payment be returned to him, for such a woman has turned out to be worth less than the price her kinsmen required for her. On the other hand, customary law also protects a woman who deserts her husband because of gross mistreatment of any sort and justifies refusal to return the bride-payment to the husband.

The prestige of a young woman is maintained through transmittal of her dowry. Her matri-kinsmen pool whatever they can afford to contribute to the bride. The couple is then called to the house of the young wife, where the ceremonial act of transmittal is clearly set forth in the short address that the kinsmen of the wife make for the benefit of the husband, who receives the inheritance into his custody: "Father of our nephew, take this livestock so that you may pasture them and have them multiply. Your children then may have food tomorrow and can pay their debts, so that the rich may not look upon them with scornful eyes, and that they may live on the same level as their equals. Take it, so that your luck may increase, and that you may live in peace of soul. We would like to see it, and it would please us much if this livestock branded with your iron should increase. Have good luck!" Such is the address recorded by Polanco, himself a Goajiro.

There is otherwise no formal public ceremony uniting a bride and groom; the delivery of the bride-payment seals the marriage in the eyes of society, although if there is a second installment to be paid and this is not delivered on time, the woman's kinsmen may take her away from her husband. The first payment, therefore, merely gives the man a provisional right to live with the woman as her legal spouse; it is the final payment that gives marriage complete legality.

The livestock making up the inheritance of a woman are mainly cattle, horses, mules, and donkeys. There are also goats, pigs, chickens, and other goods. But the greatest importance is attached to the larger animals. The woman's husband brands these animals (as well as the ones his wife received before her marriage) on the hindquarters with his mark and with the wife's brand on the forequarters. He is only the custodian of the herd, but his family enjoys its immediate benefits.

During the first weeks and months after the wedding, the husband has to "show respect" for his parents-in-law. He visits his wife in her mother's house and leaves her again in the morning. Also, the young wife pays visits to her husband's kinfolk and brings small presents for her parents-in-law. Through increased contact the in-laws gradually come to know each other. Gradually residence assumes a uxorilocal pattern for at least the first few years, especially if the wife's family is wealthy enough to give the young couple financial assistance.

The married couple's eventual settling down in co-residence and the birth of their first child mark the actual reinstatement of the woman within her matrilineage. She was separated from childhood on the day of her first menstruation and the ensuing puberty ceremonies. During the following marginal period, the blanqueo, she acquired the new status of an adult woman. In her newly acquired position of reinstatement, her matri-kinfolk have made it possible for her to return to the lineage that which she had received from them during childhood: the casta's life and culture. She will pay this debt by being a wife and mother. She will employ both magical means and personal charms to the best of her ability to avoid disaster for her casta, such as might be caused by barrenness, quarrels, and divorce —in short, anything that might give her husband's matri-lineage a legitimate claim for partial or complete repayment of the bride-wealth it has vested in her.

In-marrying relatives are known among the Goajiro as keraɨ. Typically, the keraɨ is forced into an arena where he is subjected to the forces of opposing allegiances: the bond of descent and that of marriage. The out-marrying male cannot actually disassociate himself from his own descent group, because he continues as their steward and defender, despite the fact that he may be physically separated from them. Furthermore, he must rely on the female lineage member of the perpetuation of his own flesh and the perpetuation of his property. As an in-law, on the other hand, the keraɨ has to become involved as much as possible in the matrilineage of his spouse because its members rely on him considerably as their immediate defender and provider. Yet, involved is not the same as assimilated. Notwithstanding any sentimental attachments, the keraɨ will remain an outsider so far as his wife's lineage is concerned.

Torn between these opposing forces, the kerai is in a conflict area *par excellence,* with a constant struggle between
reason and sentiment.

In times of open warfare, the kerai may be disposed to
defend his wife's descent group against any aggressor. Since
this is equivalent to defending his own family of procrea-
tion, the kerai will normally find this role as defender easy
to assume. However, true calamity ensues if the enemy
turns out to be the kerai's own paternal kinsman (of the
matrilineage of his father) or, worse still, a maternal kinsman of his own sib affiliation. Should either be the case,
the kerai is expected to assume the active role of mediator
for peace so long as there remains a spark of hope for peaceful settlement of the dispute. If he is fortunate, he may
receive reinforcement from a third but neutral descent
group, with kerai individually related to one of the opposing parties.

When a girl finally has become a wife, she takes full
charge of domestic affairs. She is the owner of the homestead, and it pays to maintain it in good order. She keeps
her husband's clothes and personal belonging in good condition.

A man may have the opportunity during his life to marry
more than one wife, in succession or in polygyny. A later
wife may be of the same matrilineage as his first wife, possibly but infrequently his stepdaughter or his wife's sister's
daughter. Marriage bonds between a man and the matrilineal relatives of his father-in-law (except when his father-
in-law is his own maternal uncle) are contracted more
frequently, because the man feels less closely related to
them than to the women on his first wife's mother's side.
If a man dies, any of his matri-kinsmen may marry his
widow (or widows) without further payment. Patrilateral
kinsmen of a dead husband would have to raise a new
bride-payment.

Polygyny is a potential danger to the women of a lineage, since the husband (under non-sororal circumstances) diverts his strength and attention to two or more matrilineages, and because jealousy among co-wives may result in suicide. A Goajiro woman will therefore try to make herself sexually attractive to her husband in order to hold his attention as long as possible. Sex education has been one of the focal points in her training as an adolescent.

A husband's happiness and his dedication to protect her and her offspring guarantee the harmonious and peaceful increment of her matrilineage. Her matrilineal kinsmen are the other arm of her protection. But the married brothers of a woman usually live away, with the families of their wives. This circumstance makes the protective power of the husband essential. Pressure is taken off the husband if, as in the case of high-ranking and politically powerful lineages, he is an heir-nephew and continues to reside with his uncle even after marriage. The husband generally maintains a cordial relationship with his wife, who in numerous ways recognizes his important position in the family. Even in polygynous families the husband remains in semipermanent residence with his principal wife and visits his secondary wives only occasionally.

The brother of a woman's husband is the "father" who will replace the true father of a widow's children. All brothers-in-law of a woman are obligated to care for the widow and the children of their deceased brothers. That is why the children of brothers are taught from an early age to be most kind toward their paternal uncle. He is like their true father to them, and they are like his own children to him. This makes any eventual change easier.

Respect and honor in Goajiro society are in large part a function of wealth. The matrilineage of both spouses will therefore bolster the position of their newlyweds by transferring to them their respective inheritance and dowry.

However, neither kind of property transaction will take place unless the matrilineal kinsmen of the spouses are satisfied with the marriage and can be reasonably sure that their matrilineage's property will pass into good hands.

Shortly before or sometime after his marriage, the husband may receive a formal inheritance from one or several of his maternal aunts or uncles. This takes place during a special ceremony in the house of the chief contributor to the inheritance, and in the presence of formal witnesses. During the festivities that follow the transaction, the young heir will leave the circle of his maternal uncles and older men and join his own peers.

Once a man has passed on to his heirs his responsibility for the matrilineage's herds and wealth, the younger generation of nephews and nieces leaves him, even during the transaction ceremony of the inheritance, to celebrate the occasion in communion with their peers. The old maternal uncle continues to have influence among his matri-kinsmen, especially if he retains some wealth. But the dynamics of the lineage now revolve about the young, the strong, the alert—the steward maternal uncle of the younger set.

For a woman, old age sets in with the menopause. As clearly as her first menstruation had marked the end of her childhood, the cessation of her menses marks the death of her womanhood. For the matrilineage on earth, she is as good as dead. Her body does not continue to produce menstrual blood to feed new life in her womb, and she has ceased to be a regenerative instrument of the matrilineage. But both the old man and the old woman continue to be of social, and possibly economic, importance. Their roles change from those of militant man and childbearing woman to a more contemplative advisory capacity. The change in a woman's status when she is past childbearing is very pronounced. This differs from the case of the man, who, when he reaches old age, does not abruptly change the configuration of elements in his life but, rather, loses some of them and adopts an attenuated pattern of social and cultural participation. The woman who has entered the post-menopausal phase becomes quite a different creature altogether. She enjoys a degree of liberty in the community hitherto denied her as a fertile woman: she can get drunk; she can smoke; she has sexual license; she does not have to comply with certain female taboos; she does not have to conform very closely to social norms; if her husband dies, she is not required to become the wife of his heir. In other words, she is detached to a great extent from control by social regimen, and she is set off in a sphere all her own, unencumbered by conventional obligations.

Old people without property are completely dependent upon the mercy of their children and other matrilineal kinfolk. As would be expected in a society where personal status is a function of relative wealth, this mercy usually amounts to nothing more than indifferent toleration of the old by the young.

Death comes as a long-expected friend to most aged Goajiro. Although their matri-kinsmen may have been indifferent during the long and often painful waiting period, they become extremely active when actual death occurs. The lineage is responsible for the proper preparation of the corpse, the funeral, and the sending of their relative on the long journey of his spirit existence.

Invitations to the wake and funeral are sent out to the matri-kinsmen as soon as death appears imminent. At the moment of death, the spirit leaves the body to bid good-by to people and places the deceased knew in life. The farewell takes place while the corpse is covered up and left alone for a short period. Then several maternal kinswomen wash the corpse and dry it with great care. Women are decorated with facial designs, which are as important for their life in the spirit world as they were for life on earth.

The body is wrapped in three large pieces of specially woven cloth; an extra cloth dresses the face and head.

The corpse lies in state in its hammock for three days. The strong bond of flesh between the dead and his living kinswomen is illustrated by the custom of slinging their hammocks close to his. Wailing in high-pitched voices, from time to time they cover their faces with a piece of black cloth and go to bend over the corpse. The casta men come from the back of the house, cover their faces with their hands, and bend over their dead kinsman.

The friends and relatives attending the wake are compensated for this service with a generous supply of food and drink. The meat is taken from the dead person's herd, and sometimes so many head are slaughtered that funeral guests can take part of their share home with them. The matri-kinsmen are not permitted to eat from a deceased kinsman's animals, for these are of their own lineage. This would be equivalent to the mixing of flesh with flesh and hence would be like incest.

As the living matrilineage boasts a material wealth of live cattle, the dead matrilineage accumulates an ever-increasing spirit herd, and score is kept of these numbers. The partakers in the funeral meals are also witness to the deceased member's value in the spirit world. After his separation from the earthly sib through death, his status as a spirit member of the sib will be established on the basis of the number of cattle and other animals that were slaughtered by his kinsmen during the wake. Inasmuch as the spirits of the slaughtered animals accompany the human spirit to the afterlife, killing of cattle in abundance during the funeral is one of the most important responsibilities of the surviving sib members. The promptness and efficiency with which this task is accomplished are far less a reflection of personal feelings toward the deceased than of the superseding interest of the matrilineage, whose intrinsic value must be established in the spirit world.

At the end of the wake, the corpse is wrapped in the hide of a freshly slaughtered bull. Arms at sides, sometimes in a flexed position, he is then buried in the matrilineage's graveyard. The grave, which is fairly shallow, has already been dug by one of the deceased's close male kinsmen, usually a favorite maternal nephew. The man who is chosen to dig the grave considers his selection an honor; to refuse this responsibility would be regarded as a heinous offense against the dead person and the honor of the lineage. Once the dead man has left his terrestrial abode through the narrow passage of the grave, the spirit, wrapped in his new "skin," assumes the form of life peculiar to the spirit world.

It sometimes happens that a Goajiro must be buried away from home, outside his matrilineage graveyard. But it is only in the ground of this graveyard that a person's afterlife can commence, and so the matri-kinsmen will see to it that at least the secondary burial takes place there. He enters the spirit world in his proper kin relationship, because closeness of flesh is symbolized spatially through the arrangement of the graves in the cemetery. His kinsmen leave food and drink, pocket money, and a torch or flashlight to give him a good start on his journey through the spirit world. The bodies of young children are buried with mirrors, so that they can look at themselves while traveling as spirits; otherwise they may get distracted on the way.

Secondary burial takes place after the body has been interred for several years. The guests are feasted again on this occasion, while the matri-kinsmen of the dead indicate their bond of kinship with him by observing the prescribed food taboos. The animals eaten are often part of the deceased's herds, which were divided among the matri-kinsmen after the primary funeral. The female animals, in particular, will still be available even after the long interval between primary and secondary burial, because no female animals can be sold.

The matri-kinsmen are responsible for ensuring the correct passage of the deceased by taking the proper funerary precautions. The party gathers at night at the site of the grave to witness the disinterment of the remains. Two close female relatives of the deceased open the grave and remove the skeleton. These women are entirely covered by black mantas, and one of them has her hands wrapped in cloth, for it is she who will scrape the dust away from the grave and recover the bones. She receives the skull first and handles it with great respect. The bones are cleaned of the remaining flesh and placed by her companion in a funerary urn.

Two or three days after the ceremony of cleansing the bones, and after they have been sufficiently mourned, the urn is taken to the lineage cemetery. Here it is buried, leaving the mouth exposed above the ground so that the soul can freely leave and re-enter.

Suicides, which are not given the conventional *post mortem* treatment, will never be able to set out on a journey through the spirit world. They have disrupted the natural cycle of their flesh and have lost their sib identification. They cannot be reborn. In their suffering they become the tormentors of their lineage kinfolk, who may have provoked them to suicide. He who dies a violent death by someone else's hand is compelled to take revenge before he can start on his spirit journey.

After the corpse has been interred, the spirit takes its spirit cattle and travels to a cave, the Jepira, on an island off Cabo de la Vega, the extreme point of La Guajira. Here it drives its animals into a corral where feed and water are abundant. It then goes to salute its kinsmen. The Jepira

enters the sea and extends transversely through a mountain. On its arrival, hungry and thirsty, the spirit is asked
by the spirits in the cave to submit to a series of tests; it
has to comply if it wants to become fit for the world of
spirits. Among other tasks, it has to eat human flesh while
it is well aware of its cannibalistic act.

The spirits of the dead float about in the cave; they
do not speak to humans who come to visit them there,
nor do they allow their faces to be seen. Children who die
young do not come to this cave. The spirits in the cave are
referred to by the general term miriyashing. They must
never be addressed by their personal names, lest they interrupt their period in the Jepira and visit the earth. The
matri-kinsmen of the dead file a claim for cobro against
anyone who mentions his name. Sometimes the dead have
to come back, which is against their interest, but they
never communicate verbally with the living except in
dreams. For instance, if the deceased is a shaman, he may
have to return in order to assist in curing. To cure a sick
person is in the interest of the casta. That is why Umaralá,
the original shaman, received his power from a deceased
maternal aunt of his. Other spirits may return to tell a
sister or niece in a dream where they have left their valu-
ables hidden. Spirits will give this information only to
their matrilineal kinswomen, with whom they remain in
communication.

Finally, after a period of months, the spirit abandons
the Jepira and sets out on its long journey, which ends
when it re-enters the uterus of one of its sibs' women to
continue the cycle of the flesh.

In several mythological versions on record, a culture
hero named Maleíwa is identified as the creator of the
Goajiro. He is depicted as a potter-creator, a creator of
man from under a rock and out of the water. It seems that
Maleíwa is not *ex nihilo* but had a mother. In the very

beginning of the Goajira genesis, therefore, there was Woman. She lived in solitude until, during one of her menstrual periods, she encountered a powerful thunderstorm and became pregnant. Her Boy Child is Maleíwa, the creator. Thus Maleíwa was born out of the eternal Woman without the agency of a man. The name of this *Urmutter* is Mother of Maleíwa.

In one version of the Goajira genesis. Maleíwa created the cosmos and all vegetable and animal life on earth. Then, in the breakers of the coastal waves, he brought to life certain female animals, which he subsequently transformed into women. He conducted them ashore, where they encountered Indian men with whom they paired off and mated. Thus each woman became the mother of a different sib group. Their flesh has been transmitted from one generation to the next, and it will continue to pass through all generations to come.

Supernatural spirits that regulate natural phenomena have to be propitiated and kept at a distance, for their interference with man and his world is dangerous. Male and female shamans function as intermediaries between man and the supernatural. They cure sickness with incantations while chewing tobacco and shaking rattles, by sucking out pathogens, and by applying medicines of many kinds. They are paid for their medical efforts and pass on their professional knowledge to successors who are willing to pay for the prolonged period of training. Knowledge and shamanic power are transmitted to the novice in a special ceremony which terminates the period of apprenticeship.

Every Goajiro who lives according to the moral code of his tribe partakes forever of the protective security of his casta. This customary casta code functions like commandments regulating personal conduct; a person enjoys eternal happiness and security within the casta as long as he obeys these rules. We know very little about the Goajiro religion, but, because the casta caters to many basic material and nonmaterial needs of the individual Indian, it is likely that the transcendental world of the contemporary pastoralist Goajiro is not very complex—less complex, in any event, than that of any of the other three types of sociocultural adaptation we have discussed, and less so also, perhaps, then that of their own hunter-collector Goajiro ancestors.

BIBLIOGRAPHY

Baranquilla, José Augustin de, *Así es La Guajira*. Baranquilla, Colombia: 1946.

Bolinder, Gustaf, *Indians on Horseback*. London: Dennis Dobson, 1957.

Gutiérrez de Pineda, Virginia, "Organización Social en La Guajira," *Revista del Instituto Etnológico Nacional*, III, pt. 2, Bogotá: 1950.

Hildebrandt, Martha, "Diccionario Guajiro-Español," *Lenguas Indigenas de Venezuela*, II, Caracas: 1963.

Pineda Giraldo, Roberto, "Aspectos de la Mágica en La Guajira," *Revista del Instituto Etnológica Nacional*, III, pt. 1. Bogotá: 1950

Vegamian, P. Felix María de, "Como es La Guajira," *Tercer Conferencia Interamericana de Agricultura*. Caracas: Tipografía El Compas, 1951.

Watson, Lawrence C., "Guajiro Social Structure: A Re-examination," *Antropológica*, No. 20 (1967), 3-36.

———, *Guajiro Personality and Urbanization*. Latin American Studies, X. Los Angeles: University of California, Los Angeles, 1968.

Wilbert, Johannes, "Goajiro Kinship and the *Èiruku* Cycle," in W. Goldschmidt and H. Hoijer, eds., *The Social Anthropology of Latin America. Essays in Honor of Ralph L. Beals*. Latin American Studies, XIV. Los Angeles: University of California, Los Angeles, 1970.

Index